Praise for Erin Weed and *Just One Word*

"I've gone through this process, and it helped me leave a past behind and step into a new future. Most books on purpose and authenticity are a bit too 'jazz hands' for me. This one delivers."

—Michael Bungay Stanier, author of
The Coaching Habit

"One word. Too simple to believe. Too powerful to ignore. I've watched it change lives. This book shows you how."

—Phil McKinney, author of *Beyond the Obvious*
and former CTO of HP

"Erin is brilliant at helping you to find your deeper purpose on the planet. I loved my Dig with her. You will not want to miss going through the Dig with her in her excellent book."

—Margaret Paul, PhD, bestselling author
and co-creator of Inner Bonding

"*Just One Word* is a gentle and powerful guide back to yourself. Erin Weed offers a clear, thoughtful process for uncovering the truth at the center of your life. She shows how one word can illuminate your purpose and help you show up with more presence, connection, and calm. This book is practical, grounding, and helps us remember who we truly are."

—Shauna Shapiro, PhD, professor, bestselling author,
and mindfulness researcher

"Your body never lies, and neither does your purpose. In *Just One Word*, Erin Weed gives you a clear way to understand the message you carry before you ever speak a word. When you know your purpose, you walk into every room differently. If you want to lead with confidence and speak with power, start here."

—Linda Clemons, body language expert
and author of *Hush*

"Capturing your life in one word would seem to be an impossible task, but through Erin's deep wisdom and her tested method, the Dig, you will unlock whole new ways to understand yourself and realize your potential."

—Pamela Slim, author of *Body of Work*
and *The Widest Net*

"As someone who coaches women into visibility and impact, I know the greatest driver of influence is who you are—not what you do. Erin Weed's method reveals that truth with stunning simplicity. *Just One Word* helps women discover the essential identity that makes their presence powerful and their leadership unmistakable."

—Claire Zammit, PhD, founder of
WomanCenteredCoaching.com

"*Just One Word* brilliantly takes readers all the way into their deepest, truest motivations or purpose and then expands outward, offering a practical path for living in full alignment with that truth. Gold. That's my one word here."

—Sue Heilbronner, author of *Never Ask for the Sale*,
coach, facilitator, and speaker

JUST
ONE
WORD

JUST ONE WORD

The Surprisingly Simple Method to Discover Your Purpose and Unleash Your Power

ERIN WEED

ALLEN&UNWIN

First published in the United States in 2026 by Balance, an imprint of Grand Central Publishing, a division of Hachette Book Group, Inc., New York.

First published in trade paperback in Great Britain in 2026 by Allen & Unwin, an imprint of Atlantic Books Ltd.

10 9 8 7 6 5 4 3 2 1

A CIP catalogue record for this book is available from the British Library.

Trade Paperback ISBN: 978 1 80546 366 5
E-book ISBN: 978 1 80546 367 2

Printed and bound by CPI Group (UK) Ltd, Croydon CR0 4YY

Allen & Unwin
An imprint of Atlantic Books Ltd
Ormond House
26–27 Boswell Street
London
WC1N 3JZ

www.atlantic-books.co.uk

Product safety EU representative: Authorised Rep Compliance Ltd., Ground Floor, 71 Lower Baggot Street, Dublin, D02 P593, Ireland. www.arccompliance.com

This book is dedicated to seekers of purpose and speakers of truth. If you've ever felt a calling to share your authentic message with the world—even if you have no idea what it is (yet)—this book is for you.

CONTENTS

JUST ONE WORD

WHAT MOVES YOU?

remembered my purpose thanks to a professional mover.

It happened about a decade ago. I was in the midst of reinventing myself professionally by selling my first company and launching a new one, and personally by ending my ten-year marriage to a very good man who was very wrong for me. Part of my life overhaul meant finding a Realtor to help me sell the house I'd shared with my husband and two kids in Broomfield, Colorado. Most people find one through friends or maybe a glossy direct mail piece, but at the time, I felt isolated and overwhelmed, so I took the path of least resistance. I called a guy whose name I spotted in an advertisement placed on the baby seat of a grocery store shopping cart.

It worked out. My Realtor was a polo-shirt-wearing, briefcase-carrying professional with a confident smile and take-charge attitude that made me feel like he had everything under control. He asked me all the expected questions: How many square feet was my property? How many bathrooms did it have? How old was the roof? He had the facts locked down. He did a great job, selling my house for a cash offer in one day.

The sale over, I started making plans to move to Boulder. This time, I did some research and hired a well-reviewed moving company. Two men came to my house to take a look at my stuff and quote me a price. One of them, an older, charismatic man with a booming voice, mentioned that he'd formerly worked in tech. I was dying of curiosity about how he'd wound up in this new career.

"I wanted to haul stuff," he said. "I wanted to move people. And that's what we're going to do for you. We're going to move you, but we're also going to *moooooove* you." He practically sang the word, stretching his arm out like he was pointing me toward the horizon. "You feelin' me? You know what I'm talking about?"

I smiled because it was impossible not to. But no, I didn't have a clue what he was talking about.

"Why are you selling your house?" he asked.

I told him that I was getting divorced.

"Why are you getting divorced?"

Oh wow, we're going there? Okay. Even for someone like me, who tends to be honest with people, this was a surprise. But his curiosity was appealing, and the question didn't seem loaded or judgmental. It felt safe to answer. I told him the truth: that I'd found myself trapped in a great life that totally wasn't right for me, and I had to burn the whole thing down if I wanted to live authentically.

"All right," he said, his face lit up with excitement. "This is not a house; this is your life. It's time to *moooooove* you forward!"

Not long after, someone asked me for my Realtor's name, and I couldn't remember it. His name had barely registered. Instead, I gushed about my mover, Frederick, and insisted on passing along his phone number.

Both men had done exactly what I'd asked them to do. So why did I have such strong feelings about Frederick the mover, and absolutely none about my Realtor?

Because my Realtor didn't make the effort to connect. His job was to sell houses, and he was only interested in learning the facts that allowed him to do that job. He had asked about my house, but he'd never asked about the life that had been lived in it. He was operating strictly from the head, not the heart. This worked for our immediate transaction, but once out of sight he was out of mind, a liability in an industry that relies heavily on word of mouth. Maybe that's why he had to pay for advertising that was usually covered up by a baby's butt.

My mover's *job* was to transport stuff from one place to the next, but he knew that his *purpose* was to help people make hard transitions, to move them from one phase in their life to the next. Not only that; he found great joy in communicating that purpose to me, as though he hoped it would give me courage as I took my next steps. He was operating from the head, like my Realtor, but also from his heart. And, most importantly, Frederick was operating from his purpose. He knew what he was here for and he communicated it clearly. And because of that, he was unforgettable. He was also an inspiration. That lightness and certainty he carried? I wanted it, too. Frederick helped me remember the feeling I was looking for.

I found out later that he discovered his purpose organically after navigating some challenging personal struggles—but most people don't even know where to begin. Their sense of self seems muddy, their path uncertain. The good news is that your purpose isn't so deeply buried that you can't access it.

You just have to dig.

WHAT IS THE DIG?

The Dig is a process of hyper-distillation that helps you name your purpose and express your message. First it will lead you to identify and articulate your human operating system (HOS)—a way of decoding how you've lived your life until this moment, which you can use as a benchmark for every future decision you make. And then the Dig will put you so in tune with your purpose that you'll be able to state it in one word.

Just. One. Word.

A single word that will become a guiding light ushering you toward the opportunities and decisions that will keep you aligned with your truth. At work, it will make you a more impactful leader, help you set better goals and manage your team more effectively, and electrify your personal brand. At home, it will deepen your relationships, clarify your communication, and help you break free from the invisible ties that threaten to keep us all living small.

Sound impossible? It's not only possible but also incredibly powerful. The Dig cuts through assumptions, stories we've told ourselves, and values we aspire to—but may not live by—to reveal what has always been real and consistent underneath. It worked for me during my time of reinvention. I built an entire business around it, helping many CEOs, entrepreneurs, and creatives increase their self-awareness and amplify their communication and reach. Over one thousand Digs later, I can decisively say that it has worked, and had life-changing effects, for every single client.

It can work for you, too.

WHO NEEDS THE DIG?

Everyone I've worked with got something significant out of their Dig. Just ask former NFL star and American Ninja Warrior Anthony Trucks. Or bestselling author, podcaster, and entrepreneur Lewis Howes. Or Digital Course Academy founder Amy Porterfield, herself known for helping people make their dreams come true. By the time they came to me, they were already millionaires. They already had huge followings. Yet they had a feeling there was more to do, and after doing a Dig, they either knew what it was or they knew what they had to do next to figure it out.

It's not just people at the top of their game—the Dig changes the lives of people who have faced profound tragedy, too. I Dug a twenty-one-year-old college student named Danny whose father had just passed away, only five years after he had lost his mother. He felt directionless—and without the anchoring from family that some people take for granted during one of the most transitional moments of our lives. The Dig clarified his purpose and brought him some much-deserved peace. His one-word purpose is "Build" and he's now a successful speaker, entrepreneur, husband, and father. He's built a life his parents would be proud of.

My own mom got something out of the Dig, too! A handful of years ago, one of my clients had to cancel her session with me so she could care for her own mother in hospice. This left me without a Dig scheduled for the day, but my parents were in town. I asked my mom if she'd be interested in going through the process. She said sure, she'd do it, and let me tell you—it changed our relationship. Learning her one-word purpose of "Connection" explained so much about our moments of synchronicity and adversity.

It's not always just one person—a private Dig with a founder of a tech company led to me Digging fifty employees at a single company. The results were incredible; everyone at the company knows everyone else's one-word purpose (I made sure of that by putting it in the org chart), and this knowledge shapes interactions, business decisions, and communication practices. It helps people understand why their coworkers do what they do, what motivates and upsets them, and how to foster better business outcomes every single day. The Dig has changed how that business operates.

I've also Dug family, romantic, and business relationships, establishing a single word for a pair of people, how they relate, and what they're here to do in this world—together.

I'll share many of these stories throughout this book. I'll tell you about speakers, authors, artists, activists, executives, entrepreneurs, people struggling with addiction, parents, kids, humans at a significant moment of transformation—and more. Some names you may recognize. They're celebrities, founders, and leaders. Others will be totally new to you. They could be your neighbor or a member of your kids' parent-teacher association. But every one of them has benefited from and been changed by the Dig.

So when people say, "Who needs the Dig?," I'll simply share the answer that comes up over and over in post-Dig interviews: everyone.

Everyone needs the Dig.

WHERE DID THE DIG COME FROM?

I didn't come to the Dig from a place of having it all figured out. Finding my own purpose wasn't a walk in the park. I stumbled on it because I was desperately hurting and willing to try (almost) anything to heal.

My first business was born of tragedy. It was 2001, just one year after I'd graduated from college and started a career in PR and marketing in New York City. That year, one of my closest friends, Shannon McNamara, was murdered in her apartment near Eastern Illinois University. As I made plans to go home and mourn her, I invited mutual friends, all of us shocked, distraught, and grieving, to join me around a campfire in my family's backyard the night before the funeral. We talked about Shannon, we talked about the as-yet-unsolved crime, and finally, we talked about our future plans.

Or rather, I heard my dearest friends in the world—all educated, strong, and smart—talk about what they *wouldn't* do.

One said that after what happened to Shannon, she didn't think she would take the hospital internship she'd been so excited about after all, because it was downtown, and she didn't think it would be safe for her to walk to her car at night. Another said that she'd been thinking of breaking up with her boyfriend, but now she thought it would probably be a good idea for them to move in together, because it's dangerous to sleep alone at night. Another friend had been planning a solo backpacking trip across Europe for months but was reconsidering.

This went on for hours. Shannon would have been so upset. She had not let her attacker take her down easily. She'd fought back hard—yet, not a week later, her friends were already submitting to anxiety and smothering their dreams.

This was a tragedy I could do something about. I started Girls Fight Back, a violence prevention and personal safety seminar production company that taught young women not only how to defend themselves but also how to resist making decisions based on fear.

I was on a mission. In less than a decade, I delivered seminars that gave over one million high school– and college-aged women the tools to protect and empower themselves. I crisscrossed the country almost daily, presenting to schools, corporations, financial groups, and other organizations. I had a speaking agent, a manager, sponsorships, and a trained staff to help me get the message to more people than I could on my own—including women in India, Pakistan, and Fiji. I was a regular on TV, the first person the networks called when yet another woman was killed. I was the poster child for women's advocacy, and people told me that my message was profound and powerful.

But the whole time I was running the company, I second-guessed myself and felt an underlying sense of anxiety and doubt, like a fever.

At first, when I tried to figure out where these feelings were coming from, I thought I was reacting to the pressure to be perfect. When I started presenting in 2001, the standard was to be polished and flawless. That was hard for me, especially in unfriendly territory, like a high school auditorium filled with girls who'd rather be anywhere else. Then, for better or for worse, the rise of reality television revealed that people actually had an appetite for authenticity. I discovered that the more raw and real I was about my thoughts, feelings, and desires, the more powerfully I connected with my audience, and the better they absorbed my message. But even then, though I finally felt free to speak truthfully during my presentations and the company was going gangbusters, things sometimes felt...off.

Twelve years later, after the birth of my daughter on what should have been Shannon's thirty-third birthday, I realized that I had crossed the bridge from pain to peace. I was ready to let go of Girls Fight Back. Before I took another step forward, however, I needed to understand what I'd just been through, and why, even as the company had become my whole identity, I'd never really felt comfortable embracing it.

I asked myself a million questions, trying to remember who I'd been before. Why had I really started this company? Why did I never feel like it was a perfect fit, even when it had succeeded beyond my wildest expectations? Why did I resist becoming the new face of women's empowerment? I dug deep. I hacked and scratched and peered into dark places of my mind and soul that I'd never really thought to examine.

I finally realized that the reason I'd been so ill at ease granting interviews to the media and being invited to events centered on women's issues was that I'd allowed the public to believe what they wanted to believe about me. For twelve years, they assumed I'd launched this company to avenge Shannon's murder, and that because I was a woman talking about women's safety, I'd naturally be interested in speaking about equity, justice, and empowerment. But though I recognized their importance, those issues didn't drive me.

What motivated my work was a deep resistance to living in a world in which women had to run their decisions through a safety calculator. To me, empowerment looked like being able to do whatever the hell I wanted—travel by myself or with a friend; live alone or with a partner; wear this sexy outfit and not that boring one; walk this interesting, twisty path instead of that straight, well-lit street—without being afraid of getting raped or killed.

I wanted women to live their truth, and I could look backward and spot the instant that I'd committed myself to this cause—sitting around the campfire in my backyard, listening to my friends talk about how they would settle and make their lives smaller so they could stay safe. Girls Fight Back had been my way of giving women the tools to kick ass so they could go out confidently into the world and be 100 percent themselves—and never make life decisions stemming from fear. **The message I'd wanted to share all along wasn't about safety—it was about being your authentic self.**

I'd built a box for myself without checking to make sure it fit me. No wonder it had always felt uncomfortable.

In the meantime, I became a speaking coach at TEDxBoulder, growing a robust client list of entrepreneurs, CEOs, athletes, and activists who wanted me to help them deliver speeches that would garner attention, open doors, and increase their name and brand recognition. They believed their experiences and hard-earned wisdom had left them with an important message to share—if they could just figure out what it was.

Despite having stacked up years of professional expertise and loads of insights and data, they were overwhelmed by the prospect of distilling it all into an eighteen-minute talk. They could list their professional milestones, but many couldn't tell me what they actually *did*. Worse, most couldn't articulate what they'd learned after nearly half a lifetime doing it.

Traditional speaker strategies didn't help much. Those were good for crafting polished presentations but ineffective for extracting the kind of deep, powerful insights that make a story memorable and visceral. I was hungry for more and believed the public was, too, so I started putting my clients through the same intense introspection I'd done on myself.

I discovered that I could ground my clients if we started from the very beginning. *Tell me, where were you born?* Their relief was palpable. Now, *that* was a question they could answer. I dug deeper. *Where'd you go to school? Oh, you played basketball? Tell me about that.*

As they narrated the facts, I could see them relax. I grabbed a pack of sticky notes and delved into their lives, writing down their ideas, feelings, and stories, none of which they thought were relevant to their intended topic. But they were wrong. Because when you Dig, a pattern emerges. Look deep enough, and that pattern will expose what means the most to you. That's where the truth lies. That's the message.

I found that the further we distilled their message, the more potent it became, until it could, amazingly, be expressed in just one word.

And as much as my early clients might have fought the process, the minute we drilled down to that one word on a sticky note, they knew it was right. They could feel it at a cellular level—one word that expressed not only what they wanted to communicate to the world, but also who they actually were. You could see the sense of peace settle over them as the ideas they'd developed over the years coalesced and clicked into place. Everything was clear. After that, their speeches practically wrote themselves.

Many went on to deliver spine-tingling TEDx Talks that inspired millions and catapulted their businesses and organizations to the next level. Some decided it was time to build something new. More than one realized they didn't want to write a speech at all, and instead dropped everything and went to Burning Man. All reported that the process they'd just been through had been transformational. They returned to their work and lives with a renewed sense of purpose, a clearer understanding of what they wanted to achieve and why it was important, and above all, how to convey that message in a memorable way to the people who needed to hear it.

And there was more: The clearer people were about their purpose, the clearer they became about everything else going on much closer to home, from why there was friction within their organizations to the sources of tension in their personal relationships. Eventually, I expanded the speechwriting business to also focus on excavating truth. The Dig process, which I initially thought was just for helping people write powerful speeches, turned out to be a process for identifying their purpose, leading to epiphanies whose impacts on my clients reverberated far beyond any TED Talk.

Discovering your authentic purpose isn't just a warm and fuzzy nice-to-have, though. It's actually a critical life skill. When you know your truth, you can more quickly identify what's going wrong when you're suffering—and figure out how to get back into a place of alignment. As you'll see throughout this book, living out of alignment with your operating system can cause incredible pain. If you're out of alignment, you may experience health challenges, bouts of depression, or simply a series of important things not working out. The Dig will give you the tools to more quickly pinpoint what's going wrong and steer your situation back on course.

That's what makes this work so incredibly important.

I'm sharing my story because I'm about to ask you to be extremely vulnerable and raw—so it seems only fair that I should start us off. One of the takeaways of my own talk for TEDxBoulder, titled "Dare to Be Authentic," is that if you want a more authentic world, somebody's got to go first. We'll get deeper into my painful, frustrating struggle bus of a journey to finding my authentic purpose as the book goes on. But for now, if you're interested in joining me, I challenge you to match this energy in your own heart. Approach this process with a spirit of curiosity and vulnerability, and you're bound to uncover something beautiful.

WHY WE DIG

I believe every one of the eight billion people on this planet deserves a chance to access their raw, authentic, most true expression of themselves and build a life aligned with it. Whether you're at a crossroads, want confirmation that you're on the right path, or just want to get to know yourself more deeply, the Dig will give you the tools to operate better in all aspects of your life.

But a warm and fuzzy sense of alignment isn't the only reason to go through the Dig. There are powerful benefits to living in your truth—in the workplace, at home, and everywhere you make an impact in your life.

You'll Become a Better Communicator
The Dig is a method for discovering your purpose and expressing what matters, and that last part is as important as the first. While empowering, it's not enough to know the truth about who you are,

why you're here, and what you stand for. In my experience, those who are living their truth almost always feel compelled to share it with the world. In large ways and small, they become beacons to those around them, shining their message and inviting others to join them in a place of truth.

One of the side effects of the Dig is becoming a better communicator. When you understand your own truth more fully, your message won't stay muddy for long.

Good communication is nonnegotiable. It's at the heart of a great life, and crystallizing your message so that it is understood—so that *you* are understood—is key to making the maximum impact on those around you. Whether you're connecting one-to-one, one-to-some, or one-to-many, getting crystal clear on your purpose helps you send a strong message in all the different ways you might speak up, share what you know, and start a conversation.

When we express ourselves poorly, we breed conflict, confusion, and apathy, which can weaken relationships, teams, and even entire communities and organizations. We experience disconnects with the people we love, with our coworkers, with our neighbors. We can even lose sight of our own truth and find ourselves living a life we don't want.

That's why understanding our purpose and sharing our message clearly and succinctly is so important; it helps us connect with people at the visceral level that's necessary for them to want to share your message, too. You sometimes see this play out in its literal form in religious faiths that encourage proselytization, or an often-quoted speech. You can also see it when a company's incredible culture invites a number of high-quality applicants and low employee turnover rates, in the loyal customer who raves about their favorite products and services (Hi, Frederick!), and in the most generous and enthusiastic donors, organizers, and participants connected to charitable or political causes.

We communicate most eloquently and effectively when we do it in ways that feel authentic. That means we have to know ourselves and what we stand for incredibly well. Knowing your purpose is nothing short of a superpower for anyone who wants to make an impact.

You'll See Your Path More Clearly

Living a more purpose-filled life may also have mental and physical benefits, helping inoculate you against stress and burnout, which are at all-time highs. Nearly 90 percent of millennials report experiencing anxiety, confusion, and even depression as they navigate the inherent changes that punctuate their twenties and early thirties.[1] In 2023, almost half of Gen Z described themselves as "stressed or anxious at work all or most of the time."[2]

But you know who isn't miserable? Entrepreneurs. In the first major study examining entrepreneurs and job burnout,[3] researchers found that entrepreneurs have a lower risk of burnout than salaried employees due to their entrepreneurial mindset.[4] Why is this?

Well, what are successful, fulfilled entrepreneurs known for? Creativity, yes. Stamina, absolutely. But they're best known for a laser-like clarity of purpose.

Clarity of purpose begets a sense of agency, which gives people the freedom and confidence to make decisions and explain those decisions to others. It allows them to act without getting mired in indecision and anxiety. And it cuts through the thorny thicket of what-ifs and should-dos and other mental traps that lead to stress and burnout.

A clear message and sense of purpose are crucial to sustaining yourself for the long haul, which is why entrepreneurs are generally satisfied with their work, even though the work is grueling, even when they struggle,[5] and even when they're not rich (most aren't).

Not everyone can be an entrepreneur, but everyone can have the clarity and agency of one.

You'll Create Deeper Connections

While the Dig may sound like a personal development tool, I've actually Dug teams—and even the entire Google Technical Services (gTech) sector—in order to help them understand their message more clearly and strengthen the bonds between team members.

The Dig is great for business. The new generation of employees doesn't want to just do their job and go home. They want to feel connected to something, and that connection has to go both ways! You can't just extract labor from people and hand them a paycheck in return. In fact, Gen Z, poised to comprise 30 percent of the workforce by 2030,[6] is the least salary-motivated generation ever.[7] What matters most to them? Authenticity. Even today, when Millennials and Gen Xers still have a dominant influence in the workplace, companies where people feel they can be authentic perform better and have lower rates of turnover.[8]

People want to feel connected. And there's no faster way to connect than uniting around a shared purpose.

This isn't true only in the workplace. Understanding your purpose allows you to show up more fully in friendships, for your family, and in your volunteer opportunities and communities. When you master the skills of the Dig, not only will you understand yourself more deeply; you'll also have a better grasp of the relationship dynamics around you and how to create deeper connections with those whose lives you touch.

Authentic culture, leadership, and vulnerability have to be modeled, whether in the office or at home. And—like I said—someone has to go first.

Why not you?

You'll Have a Custom Map to Success

The Dig is a concrete, step-by-step process that produces a more custom-fit personal assessment better than any business coaching you can buy. After uncovering your operating system and Dig word, you'll identify clarifying questions and answers that help you live in alignment with your purpose. That alignment creates a rewarding path toward success, happiness, and fulfillment. You'll be compelled to use your Dig word as a mantra, a touchstone, and even an identifier as you navigate the rest of your life and career. Whether you're creating products, providing services, or simply interacting with the world, keeping this word in focus and making sure you're living true to it will help you do what it is you're here to do.

You can rely on your Dig word to forge a clear, direct line to your biggest hopes and dreams while staying true to your authentic self. As one client said after figuring out how to meld two distinct interests into one business idea, "The Dig let me stand fully in who I am." That level of authenticity will usher you toward the life you're supposed to lead. I've seen it over and over again.

Some people chafe at the prospect of whittling down their entire essence into one word. Surely humans are more complicated than that! Well, we are—but our purpose isn't. When we find ourselves in conflict, when we flounder, when we're frustrated or confused, however knotty or nuanced our situation may be, our struggle is ultimately a matter of misalignment. The parts of our lives that aren't aligned with our purpose are a source of friction and resistance. It looks like repeatedly having to explain yourself. It looks like constantly trying to "make it work." When we're in alignment, communication is fluid, problem-solving goes smoothly, and obstacles can be turned into opportunities. It looks like camaraderie and high morale. It feels satisfying and fulfilling. Everything is clear, even if it isn't always easy.

WHAT YOU'LL LEARN

This book will guide you step by step through the Dig, helping you understand why you're here and the message you want to share, so that you can realize your full potential and achieve everything you set out to do. Unlike books that promise to help you seek out your passion, this one turns the exploration inward, because the answer to all your questions can actually be found right there in the data of your life.

In part 1, "Set Your Foundation," we'll begin by discussing the principles behind the Dig process, helping you get in tune with your truth and filter out the noise so that you can clearly hear what your story is trying to tell you. We'll learn about the Three C's, exploring how gaining epic *clarity* in your message will help you communicate with *confidence*, leading to a greater *connection* with those around you. We'll also learn to tap into one of your most powerful tools—your intuition, or Resonance Meter—in order to access your truth and navigate the world around you with more ease. Then we'll discuss how to tap into your three centers of truth—the Head, Heart, and Core—and I'll teach you an exercise that will give you the confidence to share your truth anytime.

In part 2, "Discover Your Purpose," we'll dive into the steps of the Dig: telling your story, remembering your human operating system, uncovering your Dig word, and writing your manifesto. Here, we're getting into the data of your life, identifying the patterns that have shaped you and the truths that sit at the very core of your being. By the end of this section you'll have your Dig word in hand, along with a deep understanding of your operating system—and the language that allows you to share that with the world.

In part 3, "Align Your Life," we'll direct this internal work back outward. We'll start by exploring what we can learn from violations to your human operating system and how to approach them with grace and authenticity. Then we'll learn ways to apply your operating system and Dig word so that you can express yourself authentically in all aspects of your life. We'll build your unique tools to help you live an aligned life while making decisions, recovering from missteps, and living authentically every day. And, finally, we'll talk about how to turn your purpose into a powerful message that moves and inspires others. You'll learn to craft your message—regardless of your chosen format—in such a way that others not only understand you but are motivated to help you achieve your goals.

Most people find that their Dig word is the thing they're here on this earth to learn and teach. Once they discover it, they can't wait to share it with the world. That has definitely been true in my experience, so throughout this book I'll share stories of former clients who have used their operating system and Dig word to grow their influence and have more impact in their respective fields.

In his book *Memories, Dreams, Reflections*, Carl Jung wrote, "The privilege of a lifetime is to become who you truly are."[9] Some might say that doing this inner work is a luxury, an indulgence reserved only for those who've made it to the top of Maslow's hierarchy of needs. In simple terms, Maslow taught that humans must first meet basic needs like safety and stability before they can focus on self-actualization. But life isn't always so linear. Many people have businesses to run, employees to manage, bills to pay, and—for many—kids to raise. It's a lot! For some, it feels like too much.

But believe me. Understanding your purpose with epic clarity actually makes things easier. Imagine how you would radiate confidence if you were grounded and secure in who you are and what you stand for. Imagine how many unproductive partnerships and how much wasted time and miscommunication you could avoid. Imagine approaching all your responsibilities with a sense of agency, not reactivity, even when the circumstances of your life aren't exactly how you envisioned or would like them to be. I don't have to imagine it. I can attest that it feels like coming home.

At first glance, you might think that starting Girls Fight Back, coaching TED speakers, and leading people through the Dig have nothing in common. But when you start uncovering the thread that ties them all together, you'll see I've always had a relentless pursuit of—and dedication to—being free to authentically express oneself for the greater good.

That is my human operating system, and whether I'm talking about the best things that have ever happened in my life or the worst, every piece of my story is shaped by this operating system and points to my Dig word: "Authentic."

Your operating system is absolutely unique. Your Dig word is completely your own. And if you're willing to do the work and Dig deep into your own story in a vulnerable way, it will absolutely illuminate an incredible new life ahead.

Are you ready?

PART I

SET YOUR FOUNDATION

CHAPTER 1

THE THREE C'S: CLARITY, CONFIDENCE, CONNECTION

It's not a secret that very few people who attend a networking event actually want to be there. All those people in one room chatting and smiling, most wishing they were somewhere else, repeatedly asking and answering questions like *"Where are you from?"* and *"What do you do?"* I've been that person. It sucks.

Then there are the exceptions, those who jump into the crowd with enthusiasm, leave the event feeling energized and psyched about the people they met and the opportunities they uncovered, and genuinely look forward to the next time they get to do it again. What makes the difference?

They knew why they were there and what they wanted to accomplish and were excited to find and talk to the people who could help them do it. I've been that person, too. It's much better. So much better that the question all of us should know how to answer before attending a networking event isn't *"What do you do?"* It's *"What are you* here *to do?"* In fact, if you can answer that question, it's not just at networking events where you'll shine, but anywhere you want to have an impact or make a difference.

Why? Because as we talked about in the introduction, when you have clarity of purpose, it shines through everything you do. When you know what you're here to do, you act with more confidence, which lets you make genuine connections rather than skipping along the surface of yet another boring conversation, desperately wishing you could wrap up the event and go home.

This purpose-driven chain reaction doesn't just happen in one-on-one conversations. Think about all the times you've been inspired by a speech, or motivated to follow someone's advice, or excited to purchase a product or sign up for a service. Remember the last book or movie that stuck with you long after you turned the final page or watched the credits roll and that you felt compelled to recommend. Why did you respond that way? Something you saw or heard touched you and drew you in. Something made you light up, decide that you had to have the product or service, support the mission, be a part of the community. In sum, you felt a connection.

Connection is the secret to getting people's attention and getting things done. When we inspire connection, we inspire action, whether we're trying to make an impression at a networking event, seeking investment partners, selling Girl Scout cookies, or sharing new ideas.

My clients who seek help with their TEDx Talks and other speaking engagements know this is true. Frequently, many who write their speeches before meeting me have already presented their material several times and not gotten the response they'd hoped for—whether it was a standing ovation, increased web traffic, inquiries for more information, or speaking opportunities in the days and weeks after. They know they're not connecting with their audience, and since they're certain the issue isn't the relevance or importance of their topic, they assume the problem is with their delivery.

They come to me expecting I'll be able to give them some performance tips that will allow them to override their nerves and bring their message home, perhaps with a well-placed dramatic pause or a new version of the "Clinton thumb," that ubiquitous hand gesture used by politicians on both sides of the aisle to simultaneously convey sincerity and strength.

They're wrong on all counts. Not only do I not offer much in the way of performance tips, but I also refer people to other coaches if that's all they want.

If you're having a problem connecting with people, whether it's one-to-many, like in a speech, or one-to-some, like in a conference room, or even one-to-one, the root of the problem isn't your delivery. It isn't your lack of confidence, either, though that's also a factor. It's your lack of *clarity*.

To connect with people—to make them feel things as deeply as you do, or compel them to join you in your cause, or want to hear more of what you have to say—you don't need to become a better speaker; you need to become a clearer person. You need to be able to answer the question *"What are you here to do?"*

To find the answer to that question, we Dig.

Because I've learned that therein lies the path to the Three C's: clarity, confidence, and connection. Epic **clarity** of purpose, which enables you to communicate with **confidence**, which fuels the **connections** that enable companies, institutions, organizations, and *humans* to thrive. By the time we're done, not only do my clients know exactly how to express their message in a way that connects with an audience; they also know how to better connect with everyone in their world.

EVERYTHING STARTS WITH EPIC CLARITY

It's said we have to love ourselves before others can love us. By the same token, we have to *know* ourselves before others can know us. That's all connection is—people knowing us, understanding us, and realizing that what we want and what they want overlap. The clearer we are about who we are, what drives us, and what we're here to do— in other words, our purpose—the clearer and more confidently we express ourselves, and the higher the chances are that people will respond and help us achieve our goals.

That's true whether we're talking about marriage or medical research. We get hired when someone agrees we'll be a great fit for the job or the company culture. We raise donations when our message touches people's hearts. We obtain financial backing when we enable our investors or funders to see the potential future we see. When we're clear and confident, we're able to reach people and spur them to action.

To know our purpose, however, we need more than just clarity. We need *epic* clarity of purpose. Clarity gives you something to talk about; epic clarity goes viral. When you have clarity, you're aware, but you're not necessarily compelled to move or act. Epic clarity compels you to move forward; it cannot be ignored. And when you move through the world with epic clarity about who you are and what you're here to accomplish, it makes you and your message impossible to ignore, too.

Ash Beckham, a leadership coach and "accidental activist," came to me when she was invited to give a TEDx Talk after gaining attention for an impressive speech she'd given at Ignite Boulder. That speech was about eliminating the phrase "that's so gay" as a derogatory term, because words matter. This time, based on her lifetime experience as a lesbian, she wanted to give a talk about how to come out of the closet. On this she was clear, but she had so many potential angles to take and so many powerful stories to tell, she couldn't decide where to start. Every time she committed to one, she'd start thinking about the others she was leaving behind, all of which were equally relevant. She was spinning, and she had less than two weeks before she was expected to step out on that very important stage.

So we started to Dig. As Ash told me the stories of her life, a theme started to appear, hovering like a virtual neon sign over the sticky notes where I jotted down vital summary words to keep track of her narrative. *Freedom.*

She never actually spoke this word, but it was strikingly obvious: In every significant moment of her life when she had the strongest, most visceral responses, either positive or negative, her emotional reaction was entirely contingent on whether the situation or new information she'd learned allowed for greater freedom or less. Not just for her, but for anyone else involved or affected. Specifically, the freedom to live truthfully.

The more we Dug deeper and examined the evidence in her life, the more certain she became that the message she wanted to share was this: that the most important thing in the world was to live freely and authentically, which means we can't be afraid to speak our truth, whatever the consequences.

I still get chills when I remember the moment that I looked across the table at her and asked, "What is a closet, really?" Without hesitation, she replied, "A closet is just a hard conversation." That metaphor became the scaffold of her presentation, titled "We're All Hiding Something. Let's Find the Courage to Open Up," which has been watched nearly three million times.

That's the difference between clarity and *epic* clarity of purpose. Ash had figured out and embraced who she was long before she met me, but the Dig led Ash to epic clarity by revealing that her purpose in life wasn't to encourage gay people to come out. It was to help everyone find the courage to come out of their metaphorical closets—to have the hard conversations most of us spend too much time avoiding because we're afraid of hurting or disappointing people, or because we know that telling the truth could change everything.

Since discovering the universality of this lesson, Ash has made the crux of her business, and her life, teaching others to live freely and true to themselves. Her lesson is powerful. In fact, not long afterward, I would remember Ash's words as I initiated my divorce, and I clung to her assurance that even though it is often painful to have the hard, truthful conversations, the freedom you'll find on the other side of that closet door will be well worth the cost.

EPIC CLARITY LEADS TO CONFIDENCE—
AND CONNECTION

Once you know who you are and what you're here to do, you can feel it in your bones. It's the kind of certainty that makes you unstoppable. Epic clarity of purpose illuminates your path, for you and for everyone around you. It's impossible to ignore.

It's how we know we have to end relationships even when it will cause tremendous pain to everyone involved, including ourselves, or, on the flip side, how we know beyond a doubt we've found our life partner. Epic clarity gives you the confidence to take a risk or try something new even if it's hard, unpopular, or terrifying—or to stay the course, which can be equally hard, unpopular, or terrifying. And the more confident you feel as you're making these choices, the easier it is to explain yourself and your ideas to others. They may not agree with your line of thinking, or even like what you have to say, but at least you'll be understood.

More often than not, however, people who communicate with the confidence born of epic clarity can be seductive. We want to hear what they have to say. We can sense the brilliant light shining at the core of their message, and we're drawn to the flame.

The confidence that comes from epic clarity eliminates the need to fake it 'til you make it—which is a relief, because faking it is *exhausting*! Instead of expending all your energy choosing your words so that you can be the most appealing version of yourself, you can instead just…be yourself. Have you ever watched someone dance with abandon or heard someone forthrightly speak their mind, and wonder what it must be like to not care what other people think? Give yourself the gift of epic clarity, and you'll have your answer.

It simply takes less effort to be our authentic selves than to try to be someone we're not, and while we may lose some people along the way, we gain tenfold. Authenticity is unique, and frequently irresistible. A lot like my client Dr. D'Anne Rudden.

Dr. Rudden, an audiologist, has spent her career treating her patients' hearing loss or tinnitus (ringing in the ears) and educating and consulting with communities and workplaces—especially within the music and construction industries—on how to implement effective strategies that protect people from damaging their hearing in the course of their work.

At the time we met, she was also a volunteer and global hearing ambassador with the Starkey Hearing Foundation, a nonprofit that brings hearing healthcare services to underserved communities and marginalized individuals. She's responsible for the kind of joyful smiles and lit-up eyes you've seen if you've ever watched a video of someone hearing a human voice for the first time. And—and this is a big "and"—she is an advanced certified yoga instructor and holistic health practitioner, meaning that in addition to established medical treatments for tinnitus, she sometimes suggests lifestyle changes, alternative medicine options like supplements, and even remedies such as sound therapy, breathing exercises, and yes, yoga to help patients manage their symptoms.

She's *also*, delightfully, the kind of person who knows how to play the harmonium—a small accordion-like instrument that often shows up in yoga classes because its vibrations and rich sounds are the perfect accompaniment to meditative chants.

Dr. Rudden was invited to speak about her work with the Starkey Hearing Foundation to a group of her professional peers at the Academy of Doctors of Audiology. It was the kind of opportunity she knew could bring visibility, recognition, and advancement within her professional world. She sought my help not only because she was a naturally soft-spoken person, but also because she was struggling to find the right words to discuss what, for her, was an extremely emotional, heart-driven topic to a scientific audience. She wanted to present a more assertive version of herself onstage and thought I could give her some performance techniques to help.

As we began our work together, she quickly realized that what was keeping her from finding the right words to express herself was her ambivalence about the format of her talk. Traditionally, professional presentations are full of dry facts, figures, and slides, and she'd been trying to deliver something that fit within the mold of what her audience was expecting. Yet while they wanted to hear about the science and logistics of using the most cutting-edge advancements in audiology, what she found most exciting and inspiring was the epiphany she'd had while doing this work, which was how giving the medical gift of hearing could improve communication and open people up to a bigger world. In her heart of hearts, she felt that only when we learned to really listen to each other would we be able to heal the rifts that exist within our world.

Dr. Rudden's anxiety wasn't rooted in doubts about the quality of her work or about knowing what she wanted to say; it was about believing that she needed to mold herself to be like her peers and knowing deep down that she just wasn't. It was an issue of identity, not content. Through the Dig process, it became wildly clear to her that it would be inauthentic to talk about her scientific work while ignoring her spiritual side, as both were intrinsic to her success.

After hearing her talk about her work and what it meant to her to comfortably inhabit two such seemingly diametrically opposed worlds, it made sense when her Dig word revealed itself to be "Limitless." With that word in mind, Dr. Rudden resolved to embrace her full self, with no limits, and present the talk she wanted to give in the way she wanted to give it. This word may not have empowered you or me the way it did her, but it spoke to her on a deep soul level that was personal to her experience. And at the end of the day, it gave her permission to craft a talk that was memorable and real.

The day she stood on the academy stage, she opened and closed her hour-long presentation by playing her harmonium, using the instrument's rich sounds and vibrations to show how the disciplines of science and spirituality—which already harmoniously coexisted within her—could be brought into alignment. She asserted there was a softer limit to where science ended and spirituality began than one might initially suppose.

Did the community reject her, or dismiss her presentation as unserious? Not at all. The talk was a massive hit with her professional audience, and Dr. Rudden, now armed with the unstoppable confidence born of epic clarity, went on to connect with thousands more, becoming one of the most popular speakers on the audiology circuit as well as a social media star, and launching a well-received podcast.

Dr. Rudden had been afraid she would lose everything if she shared her truth. In the end, by unapologetically giving herself permission to claim her authentic self and insisting on a life without limits, she gained everything. She found epic clarity of purpose—to help people embrace their full, limitless selves—which gave her the confidence to present her own full self in her speech rather than fitting into the "professional" box she believed the scientific community demanded of her. And that confidence forged real connections with the people she was trying to reach.

You, too, can tap into the Three C's to share your message. Epic *clarity* makes you unshakable. Not by eliminating fear but by giving you something more important—intentionality—and grounding you in *confidence* and certainty about who you are and why you've chosen a particular path. And when you approach the world as your authentic self, it sparks the authentic *connections* that propel our ideas, our careers, and even our lives forward.

What are you waiting for?

AUTHENTICITY VERSUS TRANSPARENCY

I'm often met with resistance to the whole concept of authenticity, especially in the professional realm. Dr. Rudden isn't unique in her worry that "being herself" would be antithetical to her professional life.

Starting from a very young age, most of us are advised to just "be ourselves," but we learn very quickly that the world doesn't actually want us to do that. Society often punishes authenticity—sometimes subtly, other times explicitly—especially when we're young, before we've learned to conform and mold ourselves into a version of us that looks and behaves a lot like everyone else. Our childhoods are filled with warnings against saying what we think, in the way we want to say it: *Pipe down. Don't rock the boat. Don't make trouble. Follow the rules. Don't make anyone uncomfortable. Who do you think you are? OMG, TMI—keep that thought to yourself!*

We learn to get along to avoid confrontation and conflict, so it's no wonder people roll their eyes when hearing that they should now start trying to be more authentic. For most of us, the risks feel too high, especially at work or around people whose support we desire.

And, hey. I want to acknowledge that the risks *are* higher for some of us than for others. You might not be able to show up at work and be open about your gender, or the gender of your spouse. You might not be able to comfortably "be yourself" if your culture doesn't mesh with the dominant one in our society.

But you can still be authentic and live fully in your truth, to whatever degree you're able.

The problem is that being real—being authentic—sometimes gets confused with being transparent. So let's break it down.

The definition of transparent is to be free from pretense or deceit. It basically means you're not lying. To be authentic, however, is to be more inclusive of the whole human experience. It means being true to one's own personality, spirit, or character.

Transparency is telling someone that you're an alcoholic. Authenticity is sharing the pain behind why you drink.

Transparency is telling your partner that you had an affair. Authenticity is saying "Even though I love you, I no longer want to be married."

Transparency is the surface. Authenticity is the depth. But the important thing is that when you're acting authentically, *you* get to choose the depth. You don't have to be an oversharer and tell everyone the intimate details of your life to be authentic. You don't have to put yourself at risk in order to live in your truth. It's okay to be an introvert—you can be authentic and still establish boundaries. All it requires is to be true to yourself and show up as you really are.

When most people think of Lewis Howes, they see his larger-than-life brand. He's a former pro athlete, bestselling author, and host of *The School of Greatness* podcast. He's also six foot four and known for being incredibly ambitious, and when I worked with Lewis on his keynote for World Domination Summit, I figured he'd want to share stories that upheld his alpha male vibe. But instead, he was deeply compelled to share the story of being sexually abused by a male neighbor as a child.

He'd never talked about it on a big stage before, but he felt it was time. And as we worked on the speech, I admired his commitment to telling it authentically. He was incredibly thoughtful about how he told the story. He told it with intention, taking care not to re-traumatize anyone in the audience, while also being as honest as possible about how it had shaped his path. And when he stood on that stage and shared his truth, there wasn't a dry eye in the house.

Lewis didn't tell his story to be edgy, or brave, or to go viral. You see, his Dig word is "Freedom." He shared it because he knew that speaking his truth would not only be freeing for him, but hopefully for other people in the audience as well.

When you look at his work with *The School of Greatness*, you can see exactly how on-brand it was for him to be transparent in that moment. What Lewis is really doing is challenging others to free themselves from whatever story is holding them back. To relentlessly pursue the best versions of themselves, and to radically give their best to the world.

Authenticity makes a huge difference, as Lewis, Ash, and Dr. Rudden can attest. It's not as if their careers were struggling when they approached me for help. You don't get invited to give TEDx Talks or to present at professional conferences without having already proven yourself. But when they rediscovered their authentic selves through the Dig, they unleashed a new capacity to powerfully connect, expand their influence, and make a difference. At the same time, they modeled authenticity to others, proving that you can earn respect and success on your own terms. The immediate effects of achieving epic clarity benefit us personally, but they can simultaneously have far-reaching implications.

FIRST SEEK, THEN SHARE

It's common for clients to come to the Dig seeking greater self-awareness and growth, and to leave with ideas they feel compelled to share with others, too.

One of my clients named Chris took things one step further and created a whole business based on his Dig word. The irony is that Chris was a bit of a skeptic in the beginning. When this accomplished, confident West Point grad and army vet walked into my office, he didn't fully believe in the Dig—which he later explained was due to not fully understanding what the Dig actually was. He was only there because he very much believed in the person who recommended that he try it, because they were sure it could help him find direction. He needed a new beginning, but he didn't know where to start.

It took me some time to earn Chris's trust and get him to open up. Eventually, I learned that he was in the middle of some big life changes. His twelve-year stint on the Denver City Council was ending, as was his marriage. As he told his story, it became obvious that service was a huge theme in his life. And yet, despite the fact that he had served almost seven years in the military and had volunteered at his local church, at a high school, and with neighborhood organizations, the Dig would reveal that his purpose wasn't just service. It was making an impact as a result of his efforts that really mattered.

Once Chris realized "Impact" was his Dig word, he ran with it. Today he specializes in helping others maximize their impact through keynoting, leadership training, and coaching. He knows and loves the feeling of doing the work he's called to do and has made it his mission to help others experience that same sense of purpose and fulfillment, too.

LET'S START DIGGING

Life is too short to live it like you're at a networking event, pretending to be the person you think others want to meet, hoping to convince them to believe in you, all while keeping an eye on the door in the hope that soon you'll be able to go somewhere else. The Dig is the fastest path to learning your truth, sharing it, and connecting with the people who align with it so they can help you do what you were put on this earth to do—all while being unapologetically, authentically yourself. Do that, and the only place you'll ever want to be is right where you are.

Leaders like Ash, Dr. Rudden, Lewis, and Chris weren't born knowing how to harness the power of *clarity*, *confidence*, and *connection*, but they now excel at sharing their ideas in any format and bridging the gap between what is and the best that can be. They got there with the Dig, and so can you.

TAKEAWAYS

- The heart of good communication is the Three C's: clarity, confidence, and connection.
  - **Clarity** is more than just knowing what you do—it's knowing *why* you do it. When you're crystal clear on your purpose, it becomes the anchor for how you communicate, connect, and show up in the world. Epic clarity of purpose is the kind of insight that moves you to action and inspires others to join you in your mission.
  - **Confidence** comes from being clearly aligned with your purpose. When you have epic clarity, you stop trying to be impressive and start being real. It's the calm, grounded certainty that allows you to speak and act without second-guessing yourself, because you're showing up authentically.
  - **Connection** happens because authenticity makes you magnetic. It builds the kind of trust that opens doors and creates lasting impact. It's how your ideas catch fire, your message spreads, and the people who need your truth actually hear you.
- Being authentic doesn't mean oversharing or putting yourself at risk—it means showing up as the real you, within your boundaries. Even in environments where it would be unsafe to be fully transparent, you can still express your truth in ways that are powerful and appropriate. Authenticity is about integrity, not exposure.
- The Three C's aren't just personal tools; they're professional superpowers. Whether you're leading a team, launching a business, or navigating change, epic clarity about your purpose gives you the confidence to act with integrity and the ability to connect meaningfully with others, transforming both your impact and your influence.

- Even though your personal truth is rooted deeply inside you, no one is born knowing how to harness this. It's a skill you can absolutely learn. The Dig process helps you uncover your deeper truth—your unique purpose—and empowers you to express it with confidence. When you align with your authentic self, you'll attract the right people, create lasting impact, and feel more at home in your own life.

CHAPTER 2

THE RESONANCE METER: TUNING IN TO YOUR FREQUENCY

Have you ever walked into a room and the vibe just felt…off? Maybe the people inside aren't exactly yelling at each other or glaring, but you can still feel the tension hanging in the air. The discomfort is palpable. You just know these people were arguing before you showed up.

Or maybe you've gone to a high-stakes sporting event—a match that's going to send one team to the playoffs and end the other team's season. No one needs to explain how this game means more than other ones in the season. The energy in the pub or stadium is so electric that you know something major is happening without anyone spelling it out for you.

That, my friend, is frequency.

Call it having a gut feeling, call it emotional intelligence, call it reading the room, call it catching vibes—as human beings, we each have an innate ability to tune in to the frequencies around us. We do this all the time, often without realizing it. We sense our coworker's or partner's bad mood even before we walk through the door. We get a spidey-sense tingle telling us to turn down a second date with someone who seems perfectly nice on paper. We meet a new acquaintance and immediately know we'll be fast friends.

I'll admit this might all sound a little woo-woo. But stick with me! If you can name even one time you've had a feeling—bad or good—that turned out to be true, you've already been using your intuition and your ability to tune in to frequencies. In his book *The Intelligence of Intuition*, psychologist Gerd Gigerenzer writes, "An intuition is a feeling: 1. based on long experience, 2. that appears quickly in one's consciousness, and 3. whose underlying rationale is unconscious."[1] It's not arbitrary or a magical sixth sense, he writes. It's a tool that doctors, chess players, tennis stars, and other highly skilled individuals have at their disposal as a result of their years of developing expertise. And it's a tool that each and every one of us can grow and develop with practice.

So let me ask you. What if you could tap into it more quickly and consciously in order to better understand those around you, and create stronger connections with them? How would that change the way you live, lead, and love?

Imagine you are on your way to a high-stakes meeting. Maybe it's with a new client, a potential business partner, or your boss. Just as you're about to open the door, someone hands you a briefcase and says, "Inside this briefcase is everything you need to ace this meeting. You'll find all the information required to identify common ground and clearly communicate your position. You'll find tools to help you see the unseen and hear the unsaid. In fact, what's contained inside this briefcase will help make you a better human, parent, partner, and friend. Do you want it?"

Imagine being able to walk into every meeting with those tools already in place. How would that transform your work life, home life, and friendships?

Now, you might be tempted to skip this chapter and get to the

Dig in part 2. After all, that's what I've been hyping, right? But the Dig is really about making the unseen seen and using your intuition. The themes of your stories, the values that drive you, the pieces that make up your human operating system, your Dig word—these are all frequencies. And one of the core skills this book will teach you is how to get better at noticing those frequencies and learn how to manipulate them.

You already have the ability to tune in to the frequencies around you. But when we train ourselves to become more aware of them and hone our ability to sense them, we unlock a superpower as leaders, communicators, and friends that lets us make faster, more authentic connections with others and with ourselves.

How? By giving us more information to work with. Think about the different perspectives of a mouse and a hawk. The mouse is on the ground, stirring around in the field in search of seeds and shoots for its next meal. But it has limited sight—it can only see what's right in front of it. The hawk, on the other hand, is perched on a snag high above the field. From its tall vantage point, it has a wide view. It can see the whole field and has a much better understanding of where the dangers and opportunities lie. The hawk simply has a better vantage point.

When given the choice between working from the mouse's limited perspective and working from the hawk's expanded one, wouldn't you choose to access as much information as possible?

This information is at our fingertips. But for us to actually do anything with it, we first have to acknowledge that it's there. We have to understand what frequencies are and build enough trust in our own intuition to know what's true without proof.

Going through the Dig is an extremely intuitive process. As you look to your past for clues to who you are, you won't have any external, objective standard by which you can measure your accuracy. No gold star, no check box. What you'll get instead, if you're open to it, is a feeling. You've had it before—it's that sense in your body that you're on the right track, or when you acknowledge something that feels good and true. Our truths are like musical frequencies that you don't hear through your ears but instead feel inside your body. You can measure those frequencies through what I call the Resonance Meter, an innate device we all have that helps us register when we're making decisions that are good for us.

Learning to use and trust this built-in tool will also be crucial to identifying and judging the potential for positive, productive alignments elsewhere in your life. The Resonance Meter gives you a framework with which to judge whether an idea, person, or situation registers 100 percent positively for you, or only partly, or not at all. Whether you're leading a team, raising a family, or simply trying to make better decisions, learning how to use your Resonance Meter will be a game changer.

If you can understand how to do this, you will become a master of people, a master of communication, and a master of leadership. You will gain the ability to tap into frequency as truth, to see the ground-level details around you, but also to get a hawk's-eye view of the bigger picture.

I'll teach you how to use the Resonance Meter in a moment, but first, let's talk more about what's actually going on when we trust our intuition. Because I promise you, it's not nearly as woo-woo as it first sounds. There's a surprising amount of data processing involved—it's just not all on the surface.

THE VALUE OF INTUITION

"I just got the strangest feeling as I walked out to my car, so I locked my doors even though I usually don't. That's when I saw…"

"Something made me call my sister that morning, and if I hadn't…"

"He came to the party with a friend of mine, but I got a weird feeling about him. So when he offered to walk me home, I told him I was getting a ride with a friend. Later, I heard…"

"Everything about this business deal seemed totally normal, but as soon as we set a date to sign the paperwork I got physically sick. I couldn't put my finger on what was wrong, but I decided to call it off at the last minute anyway. That's when I found out…"

In his groundbreaking book, *The Gift of Fear*, Gavin de Becker makes the case that intuition isn't something to be dismissed as "coincidence" or outlandish. Instead, it's a cognitive system that works so quickly we dismiss it, because we can't see the step-by-step process that led to the conclusion. "We think conscious thought is somehow better," he writes, "when in fact, intuition is soaring flight compared to the plodding of logic."[2]

I first came across de Becker's work when I was running Girls Fight Back, and I found it to be an excellent framework to help women develop their innate abilities to predict whether a situation or person is dangerous—because so many of us dismiss our instincts as "having a feeling," when instead we're simply processing the signals around us at a much faster pace than our conscious brain can keep up with.

While many of the examples in de Becker's book have to do with surviving (or avoiding) violent encounters, he also shares a story of dining out with a friend to illustrate this point. Off the cuff, he guessed that their waiter was actually the owner of the restaurant, that he was from Iran, and that his family owned a series of successful restaurants before moving to the US. But on further reflection, de Becker studied the clues around them—such as the man's demeanor and the prominent elephant theme in the decor—and decided to change his characterization of the man and his business. He was actually from India, de Becker decided.

At the end of the meal, he asked the man about his background. It turned out that de Becker's first lightning-flash "guess" was completely accurate, even though he couldn't point to concrete proof of why his instinct was right. His slower "reasoned assessment" was completely off base.

We naturally tap into the frequencies that surround us, the invisible radio waves of energy that everyone in our vicinity is sending out. Every animal does this; it's part of our evolutionary drive for survival. For millennia we have learned to instantly recognize signs of danger, safety, friendship, welcome, and ill intent. If our ancestors had stood around and wondered if they were "just overreacting" about that rustle they heard in the bushes, they wouldn't have survived to pass on their genes.

Yet we, as modern humans, train ourselves to discount those signals all the time. It's not just a matter of getting in an elevator with a lone stranger even though every fiber of our being is screaming to wait for the next one. We say yes to clients and projects our bodies are loudly yelling for us to say no to. We justify not reaching out to someone even though our gut tells us to make a call. We agree with the group consensus even though something feels off.

When things go wrong, we tell ourselves that "hindsight is twenty-twenty and there was no way we could have known." But if we dig deeper, we often realize that we *did* know all along. We just ignored our feelings because we didn't have proof to back them up, or we didn't want our first instinct to be true for some reason.

When I talk about tapping into frequencies, what's going on is that we're picking up on unspoken signals and environmental cues. We're recognizing patterns. Sometimes, when we go back and think through the events that led up to our "weird feeling," we can identify many of those signals. Other times we can't—but that doesn't mean the signals weren't there. It's as if our bodies are equipped with an internal Resonance Meter, picking up on these unseen frequencies to guide us toward safety—or away from harm.

In 2014, the Office of Naval Research launched a four-year study of intuition after hearing reports from soldiers in the field describing a "sixth sense" that warned them of attack. Calling it "sensemaking," they concluded that the "precognitive" ability of some soldiers is something that can be studied, as well as taught to other soldiers.[3] These low-frequency signals—discomfort, unease, manipulation—warn us about danger. They tell us something is out of alignment. The trick is learning to trust those signals.

The work of Dr. Joe Dispenza dives deeper into understanding the science behind the frequencies of the world around us and how they interact with our minds and bodies. In his bestselling book *Breaking the Habit of Being Yourself* he shares his research on brain wave frequencies, which suggests we are constantly tuning in to—and influencing—energetic states through activities like meditation and focused intention.[4]

According to Dr. Dispenza, our hearts and brains both produce electromagnetic fields that influence each other and can even extend outside the body. When the heart emits a coherent (stable and rhythmic) signal, there are signs that it has a positive impact on brain function and body regulation. When it emits an erratic, disordered signal due to negative emotions like fear, stress, or anger, it can have a negative impact on other organs—including the brain. This can help explain why cultivating elevated emotions like gratitude or joy through practices such as meditation can make real physical changes in the body.

What we feel energetically not only reflects our reality; it can shape it.

Storm is one of the most fascinating people I've ever taken through the Dig. He's lived what feels like twenty lives—sculptor, surfer, serial entrepreneur, e-bike disruptor. He's also on the autism spectrum, which, for him, shows up in his drive for clarity and precision and in his complete lack of tolerance for bullshit.

So I was a little bit worried when his partner called me up to suss out if the Dig would work for him. She wondered if I would be able to handle how direct Storm is. I worried that he might find the Dig too woo-woo to be useful.

We decided to go ahead with a private session—and that's when I realized how Gavin de Becker's work on intuition applied here, too. What I viewed as tuning in to frequencies, Storm viewed as compiling data. He found great comfort in the documentation of stories and cataloging of words and repetition, of sifting through the data points of his life to identify the recurring patterns within. We all experience intuition differently.

Storm's Dig word is "Live," and every chapter of his life is a full-bodied expression of that word. Whether he's sculpting, surfing, or launching a new product, he lives fully. His frequency is about seizing the day and doing whatever the hell he wants—boldly, curiously, and unapologetically. He does this intuitively, just sources the information from a different place.

Tapping into frequencies isn't just about sifting through data on a personal level. You can't get more data-driven and less woo-woo than a big tech company—and that's exactly what I went up against when I Dug an entire sector of Google.

The sector was Google's Technical Services team (also called gTech). It's the human support side of the company—the people you don't usually think about when you think of a high-tech, data-driven company like Google. They'd asked me to come in because the sector didn't quite match what the larger company was known for, and they realized they were attracting a lot of the wrong talent. Their goal was for me to unearth language they could use to explain succinctly what they did so they could do a better job recruiting team members who were a good fit.

In other words, gTech's team was looking for epic clarity of purpose, which would allow them to speak confidently about who they were, in order to create connections with the right kinds of people who would help them further that mission.

There are those Three C's again!

Over the course of several months, I led multiple Dig sessions with teams across the world: one-on-one interviews, small-group discussions, large, global, virtual meetings. I asked them about their job. What did they do? How did it fit in with the rest of Google? What made it so important? No matter the time zone, the role, or the team, the same words kept surfacing: "service," "support," and "customers." But, ultimately, the one that rose to the top was "human."

I remember sharing that with my main contact on the team. I was worried—"human" felt far too woo-woo a word for a company like Google. But it wasn't just my gut that told me it was the right choice. It was simply the most recurring word in all the many months of interviews I'd done. Everyone on the gTech team was expressing the same frequency.

When I shared the word with my contact, Maeve, she nodded slowly. "Of all the words in the world to choose," she said, "I never would have chosen 'human.' But it makes sense. That's who we are— the human side of Google."

When I look at someone's stories and I see a word pattern emerge, I'm not formulating opinions out of thin air—I'm collecting data points. Trusting your intuition might feel mystical at times, but it's absolutely methodical. And that's what makes it work.

LEARNING TO TUNE IN
TO THE POWER OF TUNING IN

After nearly every speech I gave while running Girls Fight Back, I had a line of people waiting to talk to me. But they didn't have questions about how to defend themselves, or what resources I would recommend to help them feel safer. Instead, they had stories they wanted to share.

As I said in the introduction, going first and sharing something vulnerable with someone—whether in a crowd or one-on-one—opens the door for them to be vulnerable in return. And when you open the floodgates of trauma for a crowd of young women and girls by sharing the story of losing a friend to homicide, you end up creating a space for them to share their own stories of trauma, abuse, rape, and murder of loved ones.

During the twelve years I ran Girls Fight Back, I was on the road constantly, fueled by rubbery airplane food and a few hours of sleep each night in an unfamiliar hotel bed. But I always made time after each speech to talk with survivors. I stood there day after day, absorbing their stories, their energies, and taking on their traumas almost as though they were my own. I was picking up everyone else's baggage, increasing my load with each presentation I gave—with no access to the tools I needed to set that baggage back down again.

Near the end of those twelve years, I was at my wit's end. I hadn't properly processed my own trauma or grief, let alone anyone else's. I was in a failing marriage. I was anxious and exhausted. I knew I was breaking, and the therapist I went to at the time essentially told me to get over it. That's when I found myself googling "psychic near me" and stumbled upon a Yelp link for Julie.

Julie had spent many years working in software before making the switch to intuitive work, so she brought a very scientific mind to her calling. When I walked into that reading with her, one of the first things she said was, "You've taken on all these other people's stories and haven't processed them. It feels like you need to let go of what's not yours. It feels like you need to heal yourself."

I nodded along like I understood, but when I got home I couldn't stop thinking about it. Heal myself? How? What does that even mean? This interaction led me to spend the next several years learning about energy, intuition, and what it means to help or teach people without depleting myself.

I studied how to tune in to the unseen and pick up on energetic truths from those around me. I learned how to understand and interpret frequencies, both within myself and in others. I experienced the power of being with a person with such presence that I could feel what it was like to be in their skin. Above all, I was developing the ability to be with people's stories and see the bigger meaning.

One of the most surprising things I learned was how often people carry frequencies they don't even realize. They might be radiating adventure or creativity without ever naming it themselves. But when someone else acknowledges it, it can feel like being truly seen for the first time.

There is a big difference between the frequencies people show to the world and how they actually feel. For example, someone might say they're doing fine, but their energy tells a different story—maybe they're masking frustration or longing. Recognizing this dissonance taught me how to listen beyond words and tune in to what's really being communicated. When someone is fully aligned with their frequency, it's like a clear signal on a radio station: crisp, honest, and undeniable. But when they're out of alignment—trying to be something they're not—it's like static. You can feel the discomfort in the air.

This spiritual time in my life wasn't just about learning to read other people's energy; it was also about getting real with myself. One of the core lessons was building self-trust—learning to believe in my intuitive hits even when they seemed illogical. That's a skill that goes far beyond spiritual practice. Whether you're navigating relationships, making big decisions, or trying to lead a team, trusting your internal Resonance Meter is everything.

What I took away from that year was this: Frequencies are everywhere, in everything, and they are constantly communicating with us. When we learn to recognize them and name them, we can consciously interact with them. Once you recognize a frequency—whether it's tension, joy, fear, or excitement—you can respond intentionally rather than reactively.

For example, say you're in a bad mood. You might think you're just annoyed with a work project, but on a deeper dive your energetic frequency is actually loneliness. Maybe you need help that's not being offered, and that's where the real frustration is coming from. Maybe working on this project has triggered memories of a friend you used to do similar work with whom you haven't seen in years. Maybe you've been spending a lot of hours in the office lately, trying to get this project done, and you're starting to fear that you're missing out on important moments in your family's life. Once you've tuned in to your frequency of loneliness, you can play along the spectrum of it and make decisions that help you change that frequency to a more favorable state.

As another example, take the frequency of awkwardness—that jarring, sticky energy that feels impossible to ignore. But here's the thing: Awkwardness isn't inherently bad. In fact, it can be a doorway to truth, connection, and even humor. I love awkwardness. It's one of my favorite frequencies to observe because it's so raw and unfiltered. It forces people to drop the masks they're wearing, even if only for a moment.

Awkwardness happens when there's a clash of frequencies—when the energy between people or situations doesn't quite match up. And while most people instinctively try to escape awkwardness, I've found that leaning into it can be transformative. It's a chance to see what's real, to acknowledge the misalignment, and, sometimes, to laugh about it.

I once coached a client who was giving a speech titled "Embracing Awkwardness," about—you guessed it—the power of awkwardness. His name is Banks, and he wanted to give a five-minute speech. Banks defined awkwardness as "showing someone who you really are without meaning to," which is a definition I've always loved.

Think about it: Some of the most awkward moments in life—like an unintentional overshare or an ill-timed comment—can become the stories we retell for years. Why? Because they're real. They're human. Awkwardness forces us to let go of our polished, curated selves and simply exist in the messiness of being alive. And when we embrace that, we can shift the frequency of awkwardness from discomfort to connection.

The same holds true for a range of emotions, whether it's tension, fear, or any other intense feeling. The next time you feel that frequency creeping in, pause. Instead of rushing to smooth it over or pretend it didn't happen, ask yourself: What's real here? What's this moment trying to show me? You might find that that difficult feeling has more to offer than you ever expected—a moment of clarity, an honest conversation, or even a good laugh. And who doesn't need more of that?

All right. Let's make this practical. It's time to talk about the Resonance Meter.

THE RESONANCE METER

The Resonance Meter is extremely simple. It's a built-in tool each of us has to help register when we're making decisions that are good for us and recognize places where we're out of alignment.

Think of the Resonance Meter as a dial that goes from 0 to 100. Take, for instance, that feeling in your body that's like a "Hell yes!" That's 100. And then there's that feeling where your whole body almost recoils in a "Hell no!" That's 0.

To use the Resonance Meter, think of a statement and picture a dial in your head. (I like to show my clients a graphic of a speedometer to help them visualize this.) Where does the needle land when you say something objectively true, like *"My hair is brown/black/silver"* or *"I am sitting in my home/a coffee shop/wherever"*? Where does it land if you think of an objectively false or offensive statement?

The Resonance Meter is basically an agreed-upon metaphor for how well something resonates. During Digs, it's useful to me as a facilitator to get feedback on the observations I'm making and see how they're landing. As you do your own Dig work, you can actually picture the needle of the Resonance Meter moving: That's a 70, that's a 10, that's a 95. Outside of Digs, the Resonance Meter can help as you go about your day and do your own work.

That's it. We're just sitting back and letting the truth pick a number.

In my experience, people tend to have pretty good access to this tool. We all understand what it means to be at 100, and we all understand what it means to be at 0. From there, all it takes is a bit of practice to begin understanding all the points in between, where things are a less obvious hit on the Resonance Meter.

When you feel a pang of discomfort or unease, pause and ask yourself: Where is this hitting on the Resonance Meter, and what does that tell me? Your Resonance Meter might be giving you a subtle indicator that someone's intentions don't match their words. Or it could be a sign that you're about to make a decision that's out of alignment with your values. On the other hand, when you feel uplifted, excited, or even deeply calm, take note. Those high-frequency hits are pointing you toward alignment and authenticity.

If something is hitting low on the Resonance Meter, it's often our inclination to change the circumstances. There is certainly a time and place to try to make things better, but what if we simply accept it instead? When it comes to trusting our intuition, sometimes things don't make sense—the truth can be wildly inconvenient! But the quicker we are to accept our truth, the quicker we can align with it.

My client Krista owns a marketing agency. Her Dig word is "Dharma." She truly believes that marketing is an expression of someone's soul's purpose. Krista challenges her clients to promote themselves like it's an offering to the divine.

Recently she sent me an SOS text—she was on the verge of firing her highest-paying client. Giving up the contract would put her company into cash-flow distress, so the stakes were high. Despite seeming like a match made in heaven on paper, the client was simply not aligning with her values. The work itself was going great, but something was simply…off.

What had started out as a 95 on the Resonance Meter had plummeted to a measly 5. It had been that way for a while, but money has a way of talking us out of our truth sometimes. On some level we all know that alignment will cost us, at least in the short term.

Krista and I met up to talk through her options. It was clear by the time we sat down together, her Resonance Meter was at 0. While she believed I was helping her make the decision about whether or not to keep the client, I knew the choice was already made. Now it was just a matter of building up the confidence to act. Sometimes we just need someone to see us, validate our intuition, and reassure us that doing the scary thing is also the right thing.

ACTIVATING YOUR RESONANCE METER

To make the most of your Resonance Meter, it's important to get quiet enough to hear what your body is saying to you and to be connected enough to your body for the message to come through. Often when we're doing a lot of thinking or intuitive work, we get in our heads and leave the body behind. But our bodies are giving us extremely powerful information, and if we don't tune in, we're missing half the picture. Instead of being the hawks up in our tree with a clear view of the whole field we're operating in, we become the mouse on the ground, trapped in a narrow line of sight.

ARE YOU OPEN TO LEARNING?

Years ago, I had the privilege of working with Dr. Margaret Paul, a therapist with over fifty-six years of experience. Her approach, Inner Bonding, is as direct as it is transformative. And it begins with intent. (First I was a client of Margaret's, then she became a client of mine—and I immediately saw how her Dig word, "Intent," was foundational to her therapeutic method.)

At the start of each session, one of the questions she asks her clients is *Are you open to learning?* If the answer is anything less than yes, she gets curious. If you can't say "Yes, I'm open to learning," then your intent isn't truly to heal or change. In these cases, Margaret helps clients self-inquire about why they aren't open and how they can shift to a frequency that allows for transformation.

Margaret understands something crucial: If we're not open to learning and being curious about what makes us tick, we're just spinning our wheels. We get stuck in old patterns. Too often, we cling to what's familiar. We try to protect ourselves from hurt by controlling things so we can feel loved.

That simple yet pointed question—*"Are you open to learning?"*— is a frequency check in its purest form. Margaret doesn't just ask if her clients are willing to receive her guidance; she asks if they're willing to tune in to a higher level of awareness and shift their frequency to a place of curiosity.

As you work through the rest of this book, I invite you to make the conscious choice to be open—to learning, to change, to seeing yourself and the world differently.

It's okay if you're not ready to hold that kind of openness. There's absolutely no judgment. In fact, in calls with prospective clients, I often find myself saying something to the effect of "Look, I really think the Dig could help you. But right now doesn't seem to be the right time. What if we reconnect in three or six months?" I've said this to an accountant in the middle of tax season. And to a bride-to-be a few months before her wedding. I've said it to people who want to find their purpose after a huge loss or trauma in their lives. Sometimes it's just not the right time. These people needed the Dig—but they needed to close a few tabs first.

This process requires an honest look inward, a transparent accounting of our life's story, and a radical embracing of our past as a way to create an authentic future. It can bring up sensitive realities that are hard to look at or accept as truth. Some people simply don't have the capacity for that in this moment. Without that openness, your Resonance Meter is just a number. It can't do anything to guide you toward alignment.

In my early days of doing this work, I didn't realize how critical it was to Dig someone before helping them with their message. I still vividly remember working with a client who just wanted a speech, without all the deep Digging work as a precursor. Mike, a well-known pioneer in the tech industry, was working on a keynote. He specialized in teaching tech professionals how to be more effective and efficient—and I suspect that desire for a fast, streamlined result was partly behind his resistance to my longer soul-dive process.

But even without formally Digging, I tend to naturally ask deep questions. Throughout the session, I could feel my inquiry style creating some tension in the room. I'm guessing his Resonance Meter was a solid 2, as he wondered why this speech-coaching session felt more like therapy. Both he and I were frustrated by the end of the session and I was pretty sure I'd never hear from him again.

Weeks later, an email popped into my inbox. From Mike.

It turned out that after he left my office, he started thinking and journaling about what he really wanted to say and why it was so important to him. By doing some self-Digging, he'd uncovered the clear core message that he wanted to build his keynote around.

The message? The importance of admitting when you're wrong.

With the reflection Mike did after our session, the clarity he found on his own naturally infused itself into his keynote. The more quickly you understand (and admit) you're wrong, he told his audience, the more efficiently you can shift course and the more effective you'll be once you incorporate that newfound perspective into your own limited one.

The keynote was a hit.

It landed with Mike's audience not because it was a popular topic and not because he delivered it with flair. It landed because Mike had unearthed a message that was crystal clear and purpose-driven, which allowed him to deliver it with confidence.

I totally understand and respect when people don't feel they have the time or space to do this deeper work. (We'll talk more soon about how triggering it can be to uncover your Dig word. It's both your superpower and your Achilles' heel, and bringing it out into the open can be incredibly uncomfortable for some people.) However, there's something to be said for the amount of ease and flow that naturally occurs when you hit 100 on your Resonance Meter.

In the next chapter we'll go deeper into an exercise that will help you tap into your truth by getting in touch with your Head, Heart, and Core. But first, let's do a Resonance Meter check on how this is all landing.

Take a few deep breaths. Clear your mind. Get in touch with your Resonance Meter. Start by asking yourself some simple questions, things that are objectively true. These will help you calibrate your body's "Hell yes!" on one end of the spectrum and "No way!" responses at the other end.

Next, start pinging your Resonance Meter with things that are less immediately clear. Start with small decisions you might be on the fence about, like which restaurant to eat at, or what color to paint the walls of your kitchen, or which shoes to wear with an outfit. Then start asking questions that have deeper importance.

Get in the practice of pinging your Resonance Meter throughout the day, assigning number values to your responses. Let's try it now. Ask yourself: Are you open to learning?

If the answer is "Hell yes," let's keep going!

TAKEAWAYS

- Intuition isn't just a hunch—it's a sophisticated, lightning-fast cognitive process that helps us assess situations before our rational minds catch up. It's a survival tool rooted in biology and experience, and learning to trust it can keep us safe, aligned, and aware of when things "feel off" even without evidence.

- We're constantly picking up on invisible signals from people and environments—but we often dismiss them. Learning to identify and name these emotional and energetic frequencies gives us language for what we're feeling and empowers us to respond intentionally. When we name the energy in a room, a relationship, or ourselves, we take the first step toward shifting it.

- The Resonance Meter is a metaphorical tool that helps you assess how aligned something feels in your body, on a scale from 0 ("Hell no!") to 100 ("Hell yes!"). It helps you get out of your head and tune in to your intuitive sense of truth. With practice, this inner dial becomes a powerful guide for decision-making, communication, and authentic living.

- To tune in to your Resonance Meter, you need to clear the noise— both literal and emotional. By simply taking a moment to breathe, you can release what's not yours, reclaim lost energy, and reconnect with your intuitive self. Getting into your body is essential to hear what it's telling you.

- Openness is a frequency. If you're not open to learning, transformation stalls. As you move through the rest of the book, your willingness to stay open will determine how deep you're able to go.

CHAPTER 3

HEAD-HEART-CORE: A 3-STEP PATH TO AUTHENTIC COMMUNICATION

One of my first lessons in being an authentic communicator came from a pretty strange place: working as a paid extra on a reality TV show.

The year was 2001. On the show, each contestant went on a marathon date with four potential matches, eliminating one person each round (often in a spectacularly dramatic way) until they found "the one." It was a fairly shallow premise, and if you're judging me for taking the gig, I don't blame you.

I was grateful for this side hustle because my day job at the time didn't pay nearly enough to cover my bills. And to be super honest, I was in my twenties and it just sounded ridiculously fun!

Ironically enough, that day job was producing historical documentaries, which were all about intellectual integrity and factual accuracy. We went to great lengths to make sure everything we presented was the truth. On the reality show, however, the producers went to great lengths to make sure everything *looked* true.

The contestants were supposed to be out on the town, having these incredible dates in swanky bars while finding "the love of their life." In reality, we were shooting in some random Manhattan bar on a Tuesday afternoon. The producers would cover the windows to make it look dark inside, then crank up the fog machines to give everything that hazy nightclub look. My job was to be in the background of these wild dates, dirty dancing with other actors while sipping on a Starbucks latte poured into a martini glass.

It was all so extremely, painfully fake. But when I paid attention to how the dates were going, I began to notice a pattern. Some contestants were as phony as the set around them. Others, though, were authentic—often with a level of honesty that was jarring in a scenario where everything else was just smoke-and-mirrors TV magic. And the more honest a contestant was both factually and emotionally, and the more they expressed exactly who they were, the faster they were able to either attract or polarize potential partners.

I have no idea how many of those successful dates went on to form real relationships, but I took away a key lesson: The more honest we choose to be, the quicker we find out who our people are. (We also find out who *aren't* our people, and that's a good thing.) Honest communication has the potential to create quick connections with everyone you talk to—whether you're speed dating, working with your team, spending time with your family, or chatting with a stranger in the checkout line. The more real you are with those around you, the more connected you'll feel.

I took this lesson about communication with me when I was speaking with Girls Fight Back in front of audiences filled with young women. I had a mission: to teach girls the skills they needed to be safe from violence. I knew the GFB message would literally save lives. But, as any speaker knows, if the audience doesn't trust you, they certainly won't listen to you. And no audience is more suspicious of a speaker than an auditorium filled with teenagers who would rather be anywhere else. Teenagers won't let you get away with anything. They will check their phones in front of you. They will roll their eyes at you. They will heckle you. And if they catch even a whiff of bullshit, they'll dismiss you completely.

One day, I was using the girls' bathroom before I gave a keynote to a packed auditorium. While I was in the stall, I overheard some of the students complaining about the upcoming assembly. "OMG, I'm so mad we have to go to this stupid thing," one girl said. "This speaker is *definitely* going to suck," agreed another. "Sooooo boring," said a third. "I'd rather be *literally* anywhere else."

Oof. My confidence took a major hit after overhearing those conversations. But when I started to look at things from their perspective, I couldn't blame them. They're forced to go to a lot of assemblies that are preachy and boring. The last thing they want to do is hear one more adult talk at them and tell them what's best for their life.

How can I turn that around? I asked myself. How could I meet them where they were, in this place where they didn't want to be listening to me? How could I take them on a journey that had the potential to change their lives?

I decided to start by being honest with them—while also calling them out in the first sixty seconds of my talk. When I went out onstage, I ditched my usual opening anecdote and dove right into my truth. I said, "I want to tell you a little story. I was just in the bathroom, and I heard you all talking about how much you don't want to be here." A nervous, slightly guilty murmur rippled through the room. I continued with a smile. "I just want to say that I get it. I've been forced to sit through many boring, pointless seminars and it feels like such a waste of time. I don't want to do that to you! So let's make a deal. You give me ninety minutes of your time, and I'll teach you the tools to save your own life in a violent scenario. Deal?"

I felt the entire energy in the room change. The audience felt seen and understood. I shared my pain and clearly laid out my goals and what was in it for them. I'd built trust with them right out of the gate, by speaking my truth.

Authentic communication can help you reach audiences, whether you're talking to one person, talking to a small group, or speaking in front of hundreds—or thousands. I've found that most audiences crave realness, whether I'm standing in front of suspicious teenagers in an assembly, teaching eager fifth graders at my son's elementary school how to give short speeches, or addressing a corporate audience conditioned to avoid anything too touchy-feely. No matter whom you're talking to, the lesson is the same: When you're honest—truly honest—you build trust. And trust is the bridge to connection.

In this chapter I'll walk you through the tool I use to quickly and authentically access your truth by tapping into your Head, your Heart, and your Core. The Head-Heart-Core method works whether you're preparing a speech, asking for a raise, making a big decision, having a hard conversation with a loved one, or remembering your life's purpose.

GETTING TO THE HEAD-HEART-CORE
OF THE MATTER

I live near Boulder, Colorado, which is a beacon for hippies and a mecca for a thing called "sharing circles." It's a type of ritualized way to share your experiences with others, listen, and connect. Let me just tell you—some people can really talk it out. Sharing circles can meander into eternity and go on for hours. One by one, each person (often with a talking stick in hand, giving them ultimate power) shares what they've experienced in differing levels of detail.

Occasionally you'll get someone, clearly out of their comfort zone, who offers a five-second reflection, then lapses back into silence while the whole group breathes a prayer of thanks for the reprieve.

Don't get me wrong. I want to hear people's truths. But when it takes a long-winded ramble to get to those truths, it's hard to decipher the nuggets of wisdom embedded in the story. Most people don't have the energy or bandwidth to take on the mental load required to pull out the truth, which means the message—no matter how profound—is ultimately not getting across.

But hey, there's good news for the mystics of Boulder (and beyond)! Big, bold truths can be communicated in a very short amount of time, with a deep sense of connection as the reward for your efficiency. The method is called Head-Heart-Core and it's the baseline for authentic leadership and communication.

Head-Heart-Core is the method I developed for unearthing someone's most candid thoughts, feelings, and desires in a short, concise format, then turning them into words. The end result is internal understanding, followed by external expression of what someone thinks, feels, and wants. When you put this all together, you have a sense of self-understanding that can now be clearly and concisely shared with someone else.

Head-Heart-Core is based on the idea that there are three places from which we can speak our truth: the Head (factual truth), the Heart (emotional truth), and the Core (desire-based truth). When you put them all together, it becomes the fullest expression of your authentic self.

Very few of us have been taught how to be authentic. Sometimes we learn as we wander through our lives, stumbling around conflicting thoughts, feelings, desires, and the ability to express them in a way that makes any sense at all. This was certainly the case with me. I was raised to be polite, and as I grew up my superpower was being a chameleon who could morph her scales to fit any setting or situation. This allowed me to move through many worlds and circles with ease, but it also made it tough to discern my own preferences from what was expected of me. Even today as a forty-something grown-ass woman, I often find myself mindlessly going with the flow in order to keep the peace, instead of aligning with my truth.

Remember this crucial truth about authenticity: It's always easier to be yourself the first time, instead of having to unwind what's not your truest self later on. As we discussed in chapter 1, clarity is also a crucial element in effective communication. When speakers achieve clarity, it naturally leads to confidence, which in turn facilitates connection with the audience. But this clarity needs to be both internal and external. The Head-Heart-Core approach allows you to get clear with yourself extremely quickly.

When most of us have something important to share with someone, we hem and haw. We start with a buffer, we pour sugar on top, we make the explanation way longer than necessary—and in the process, we can utterly confuse the other person. Like those rambling souls in the oversharing circles, we barricade our true selves using a wall of filler words.

Kids are not like this. When my daughter was five, she went through a phase where she was totally opposed to footwear. Phoebe was anti-sandal, anti-sneaker, and anti-anything that would separate her soles from the earth. As much as I admire her resoluteness, we live in a shoe-loving society. The constant fight to get Phoebe to put on her shoes when we left the house made that chapter of single parenting even more challenging.

But you know what was *not* challenging? Understanding how she really felt about shoes. Why? Because she was so clear, and she naturally spoke from the Head, Heart, and Core. She said, "Mom, shoes hurt my feet. When I put them on my feet sweat and slip inside of them. It feels gross. I'm not gonna wear them."

With the exception of the highly inconvenient conclusion, it's pretty much a perfect Head-Heart-Core soliloquy. She dished out the facts, she shared her feelings, and she stated her desires. Each was no more than a sentence or two long. And while I could argue and disagree, I was never unclear about where she stood on the issue and why.

HOW REAL DO YOU WANT TO BE?

The Head-Heart-Core framework isn't just for five-year-olds. This method has been proven at companies like Google, where I have taught and even certified leaders to facilitate it for their teams. Googlers value authenticity, but their lives are also scheduled down to the minute and they don't have time to waste. So it's all about getting real…fast.

But first you need to ask yourself, "How real do I want to be?" This is an honest and necessary self-inquiry before attempting Head-Heart-Core. It's okay to say "Not very." Living in your truth doesn't mean you have to bare your soul to every person who crosses your path. Recently I was on an exhausting business trip where I was with groups of people nonstop for several days. By the end of the trip, I found myself in yet another Lyft driver's back seat. As he launched into questions about my childhood, ready to get his chat on, a wave of pure dread rushed through me. I thought, *I simply cannot connect with one more human right now.*

I wanted to be real with him but was too tired for chitchat. So I chose to stay in my integrity around this by using Head-Heart-Core. I told him the facts (I'd had a pretty intense trip and my social battery was low), my feelings (I was emotionally exhausted), and my desire (I'd be so grateful to have a quiet ride).

Upon receiving my short, direct, clear, and kind expression of where I was at, he happily obliged and we cruised along in blissful silence. And the best part? This interaction had no negative impact on my Lyft rating!

In general, it's been my experience that the more real we are—first with ourselves, then with others—the better things turn out. Sure, ghosting or avoiding or dodging or placating might feel like the more ease-filled or polite option in the moment, but given the mental load they create, it's often not best for everyone in the long run.

TAPPING INTO YOUR HEAD, HEART, AND CORE

The basis for this system is that there are three distinct aspects of your truths, and to live authentically, you need to access and understand each of the three.

- **Head (Factual Truth):** These are intellectual and indisputable facts about you or the situation at hand. Factual truths ground you in reality. They remind you who you are and clearly state what is going on. For example, "I've been working in my current role for five years" or "We haven't seen much of each other recently."
- **Heart (Emotional Truth):** This is your internal landscape. Emotional truths help you tune in to how you're experiencing the present moment and allow you to name and process feelings like joy, sadness, frustration, or hope. Unlike factual

truth, emotional truth is fluid, can change frequently, and is deeply personal and unique to you. For example, "I feel stuck in my career" or "I feel lonely and disconnected from you, and I miss spending time with you."

- **Core (Desire-Based Truth):** These are your desires and wants. Core truths articulate what you fundamentally seek in life, relationships, or experiences. For example, "I want to create work that inspires others" or "I want us to do something fun together once a week."

The Head-Heart-Core framework isn't just a communication tool—it's a lens for understanding ourselves internally first. From there it helps to improve our relationships and create a healthier, more connected society. When you integrate all three parts of yourself, you get a clear, concise picture of who you are and what matters. Each of the three truths brings something essential to the table: Factual truths provide the structure, emotional truths bring depth, and desire-based truths offer direction.

This is why it's so important to include all three. Most of us find it easier to access one aspect over the others, but when we lean too heavily on one truth or leave another out entirely, we miss opportunities for clarity, connection, and transformation.

Let's explore each truth more fully and learn how to put this into practice.

Speaking from the Head: Factual Truth

The Head focuses on sharing factual, intellectual truths. It fills in the blanks of the sentence "I know _______." Statements from the Head are indisputable facts about oneself or the topic at hand, which are important because they offer context, context builds trust, and trust builds a foundation for connection. When you're sharing from the Head, what you're really doing is providing a way for someone to be able to place you. A great example of this is one I've already picked on: the networking event. At most events, your goal is to show up, slap on a name tag, and start sharing facts—starting with the two biggies: *"Where are you from?"* and *"What do you do?"*

It gets annoying to say, "Hi, I'm Jenny from San Diego and I'm a civil engineer," again and again, which is one reason people find networking events so irritating. But the intention behind these questions, as superficial as they are, comes from a place of wanting to establish connection. People are trying to figure out (literally and figuratively) where you are in the world and how they can meet you there.

These Head facts can create instant connection. You know that feeling when you meet someone in the wild who's from your hometown? It's cool, right? Maybe you both know the same people. Maybe you went to the same high school. Maybe you both were regulars at the best townie bar at some point in your youth. (If you're from Schaumburg, Illinois, like me, we're definitely gonna bond over some shared memories of Easy Street Pub.) Location reveals potential commonalities while removing some of the mystery about this stranger you've just encountered.

Revealing what you do professionally does the same thing. For better or for worse, how we spend our days in the workplace says something about us. It lends insights into our interests, who we interact with, or if we even enjoy interacting with people at all! I've met plenty of computer programmers at networking events who've made it quite clear from the look on their faces that they're attending under duress.

Examples of Head truths include:

- "I was born in 1977."

- "I graduated from college."

- "I'm a dog owner."

- "I go hiking in the mountains on weekends."

- "I'm a fan of eighties music."

- "I drive an electric car."

Speaking from the Head helps establish a foundation of trust and provides context for deeper communication. However, relying solely on facts to fuel a conversation can start to feel flat or disconnected. As authentic leaders, if we want to connect with people on more than a surface level, we need to do the brave thing and "go first" when it comes to going deeper … and drop down into the Heart.

Communicating from the Heart: Emotional Truth

The Heart involves sharing emotional truths, which are highly personal and constantly evolving. Speaking from the Heart is vulnerable. It creates a deeper connection with your audience—but it also requires you to be tuned in to yourself, which can be difficult.

To make matters worse, most of us have been taught that Heart truths have no place in professional spaces or conversations. So much of the polarization in our society is a by-product of bypassing the Heart and oscillating between the Head ("Here are the facts") and the Core ("Let's take action"). It completely skips past the center of our physical existence and misses a huge opportunity for connection.

Emotions are a human unifier. Each of us understands what it is to feel excited, proud, and satisfied; we also understand what it is to feel hurt, anxious, lonely, or afraid. When we are vulnerable with others and share our Heart truths, we invite them to drop their barriers, too. The result is a much faster connection than if we stayed in the Head.

When accessing your Heart, I recommend first taking a deep breath to create space to really feel your feelings and drop into them. Emotions are fleeting and ever-changing, so you need to be extra present when trying to access them. Let yourself feel whatever you feel, without censorship. Too often we restrict our emotions or try to talk ourselves out of them, which stifles our truth. The end result? We get resentful because we're living a life that's woefully misaligned.

Examples of Heart truths include:

- "I feel overwhelmed by the number of tasks on my plate."

- "I'm nervous about speaking in front of this audience."

- "I'm sad about the loss of a loved one."

- "I'm hopeful for what the future holds."

- "I feel disconnected from my community right now."

- "I'm proud of what I've accomplished this year."

- "I'm scared of making the wrong decision."

- "I'm disappointed by a recent setback."

This type of sharing can be powerful but potentially exhausting if overused—or used without the guardrails of the Head and the Core. I have worked with many activists who end up burned out after operating from a place of passion for so long, especially when it's tied to a deeply emotional reason for doing the work. This can lead to fatigue and bitterness.

Staying focused on the Head and Heart alone can also leave your audience thinking, *Okay, but so what? What am I supposed to do with all these facts and feelings?* That's where the third aspect comes in. We need to tap into the Core.

Expressing from the Core: Desire-Based Truth

As the Spice Girls said, "So tell me what you want, what you really, really want"—as if this was an easy thing for everyone. For most of us, it's just damn hard. If you're a part of any marginalized community, perhaps you got the message (directly or indirectly) that you don't deserve to want anything, let alone actually get it. Or maybe you struggle with self-worth, or receiving in general. When I have done this exercise with coaching clients or in workshops, many people have told me that they were afraid about this part of the exercise because they didn't want to make someone else feel bad by claiming what they wanted.

These fears stem from the zero-sum game our culture preaches: If I get what I want, you lose out on what *you* want. I suppose if you're playing a competitive round of musical chairs, this may be true, but in most other situations in life, sharing our desires may actually allow for more abundance for all, rather than less.

When I do this exercise in person, this is the moment when I notice the room gets super energized. Rather than coming across as selfish or greedy, when people get honest about what they want and share it with each other, things come alive. For some, asking for what they want is liberating! For others it's terrifying. Either way, it's helpful to tap into your Resonance Meter when summoning your Core truth. It's a straight line into the future you desire, and an invitation for others to join you there.

Your Core truth is usually the action-oriented outcome of what's factually and/or emotionally true. It answers the question *"What next?"* or *"What now?"* and provides a sense of vision or forward momentum. It is the moment in Martin Luther King Jr.'s famous "I Have a Dream" speech when he shifts gears from laying out the facts of historic oppression and the feelings of those fighting for racial equality, to sharing a series of short, powerful desires for a better future for all.

The Core represents one's fundamental desires and wants. When communicating from the Core, statements tend to be shorter and more direct.

Examples of Core truths include:

- "I want to create meaningful work that impacts lives."

- "I want to strengthen my relationship with my kids."

- "I want to travel and experience different cultures."

- "I want to be financially secure."

- "I want to feel less stressed and more balanced."

- "I want to make peace with my past."

- "I want to simplify my life."

- "I want to see justice in the world."

There is power in our Core truths, and tapping into them can be transformative—for ourselves, for our relationships, for our communities, and for our world.

PUTTING IT ALL TOGETHER

Now it's time to put it all together in a short exercise that you can use anytime, anywhere. I'll talk through how to do this on your own for now, and then we'll talk about how to use this with a partner or in a workshop.

This exercise can be used to inform solo decisions, one-on-one communications, one-to-some small-group interactions, and one-to-many broadcast opportunities like speeches or webinars. I often recommend to my clients that when they have something they need to decide or communicate, just draw three boxes on a piece of paper and fill in the facts, feelings, and desires in each. Often at the end of this quick exercise you'll have a deeper self-understanding and more clarity on how to share it.

Start by thinking of a question to ponder, a conversation to strategize, or a decision you're wrestling with. Then you'll go through three rounds exploring each category of Head, Heart, and Core, respectively. You can speak your answers aloud, in which case you'll just need a timer to do this exercise. Or, if you like, you can type or write your answers. Choose the way that helps you think the most clearly, then find a quiet place and let's get started.

Round 1: Head

Start by framing your topic. Speak it aloud or write it at the top of your document. Then set a timer for sixty seconds and write, type, or speak all the factual truths about your question or situation.

Round 2: Heart

Now we'll drop down into the Heart and tap into our emotional truth by taking some deep breaths. Then set a timer for ninety seconds and share everything you feel on the subject. Remember, there are no rules here! Bring your anger, sadness, frustration, and everything else that is bubbling up.

Round 3: Core

Finally, set a timer for sixty seconds and tell the world what you really, really want.

Undoubtedly you'll encounter resistance in at least one of these categories. It's okay—that means you're doing it right! Push through any conditioning that might be stifling what's true for you and really let it rip. If you're still having trouble accessing those truths, try coming at it from a place of curiosity at first. Ask yourself, "What would I say if there were zero filters on?" That's probably your honest truth that doesn't feel safe to be expressed.

When doing this exercise, always go in this order. Following Head-Heart-Core creates a logical build, beginning with the factual truth. If you start out by sharing what you want—your Core truth—it lacks context. Plus, you're probably not going to be able to access that truth straight out of the gate without exploring your Head and Heart truths first.

This goes for using this method in a presentation or conversation as well. Your audience will be more receptive to the emotional truth once the factual truth has been laid out. And once the Heart truth has been communicated, people will be more open and receptive to Core truths about what needs to happen, or what you want to happen.

Go to erinweed.com/justoneword for a free training video and worksheet, where I'll walk you through an interactive Head-Heart-Core exercise. You literally have to do nothing other than watch the video and follow my instructions—easy-peasy!

HEAD-HEART-CORE
IN REAL LIFE

Recently, I gave a keynote about Head-Heart-Core at a retreat. The session was filled with coaching professionals who'd achieved great things by society's standards but who had come to the retreat to learn how to show up more fully as themselves in a world that didn't always seem to value authenticity. (Because this exercise tends to get quite personal, I have changed some details to protect participants' anonymity.)

After explaining the Head-Heart-Core exercise—just like I have for you here—I invited two people I knew would be good sports to come onstage and demonstrate for the group.

I set a timer for one minute and asked Geraldo, an entrepreneur, to begin.

He placed a hand on his head. "My name is Geraldo and I was born in Mexico, where I grew up with seven siblings. Now I live in Colorado." His voice was steady as he continued sharing facts about the businesses he'd started, the jobs he'd worked, and his schooling; he wavered only slightly when sharing facts about his children—especially about his son's struggles with mental illness.

When the minute was up, I simply said, "Thank you for sharing." Next, I asked him to take a deep breath, put a hand over his heart, and feel into what was alive for him in that moment.

"I'm feeling love," he began, smiling at the other participants in the room. "I'm feeling friendship. I feel seen." He took a breath. "I feel confused about the future of the planet. I have been feeling like I am a messenger of hope, and I should bring hope to people—and I can't allow myself to doubt, but I'm upset about the polarization of our world."

He continued. "I'm also grieving. I lost my mom a few months ago to brain cancer. I'm scared about losing my son to mental illness.

I have always traveled so much for work, and I wasn't there for him when I needed to be. Sometimes it feels like I've failed him."

When the timer went off, I thanked him again for sharing, then asked him to drop his hand to his belly, center himself, and tell us what he truly wanted—not the story, not the justification, just the desire.

He didn't hesitate.

"I want to have great sex again," he said with a grin, which drew laughter and applause. Then he grew more serious. "I want the world to be more compassionate. I want peace. I want my sons to grow into extraordinary men—good, safe, thriving people. I want everyone here to be madly in love with their lives. And I want to feel madly in love with mine again."

He paused. "I think I'm done."

Next, it was another entrepreneur's turn. As with Geraldo, I asked Jim to place his hand on his head and begin speaking from his factual truth.

Jim started with family—his wife, the children he has from his earlier marriages, his stepchildren, and his growing roster of grandchildren. He then moved on to his schooling and early years: military school, college, sports, civil rights work, doctoral studies.

The timer beeped. He laughed. "Good," he said. "What a relief, that was a lot."

Despite his relief, the facts of Jim's life had flowed easily—he'd clearly told his story countless times before. I thanked him, and Jim moved his hand to his heart and began. His tone changed immediately.

"I'm moved by what Geraldo shared," he said. "I feel love, compassion, and…sadness for what you were talking about with your son." He went on to share a painful moment he was going through with one of his own children, opening up about his fears for their future and his own worries that he hadn't been around enough for his family.

"I've been feeling tired lately," he went on. "I think I'm tired of working on Zoom, saying the same thing over and over to new groups. I want to study more and follow my inner guidance."

When he finished, I thanked him again and asked him to speak his Core truth.

"I want to lose twenty pounds," he said immediately. "I want to finish writing my book. I want to work less and make more money. I want to stop sitting on a computer all day. I want more live trainings like this—I really miss it."

Then his voice grew softer. "I want to see the polarization in the world begin to dissolve. I want more peace. More joy. More fun. I want to beat my wife at Scrabble—at least half the time. I want more time with my grandson. I want to play. And I want to drink good wine without waking up the next morning regretting it."

He looked at me and said simply, "That's it."

And just like that, we all witnessed someone who'd spent decades as a leader in his industry—someone who knows how to present himself flawlessly in public—strip away all the armor and share clearly and concisely what he wanted.

After our live-onstage guinea pigs had wrapped up their stories, I invited the audience to pair up and led them through the same exercises. I wanted people to actually experience the Head-Heart-Core framework for themselves, and the stories that arose were incredible.

One person raised a hand and told us, "I've been dreading having a conversation with my sister for six or seven years—maybe longer. But doing this exercise made it actually feel possible. Easy, even. I think…I'm going to have it."

Another participant said, "I've been needing to have a conversation with the president of my company. It's a big one. And this exercise helped me rehearse it—not from anxiety, but from truth. And now I'm ready."

One of my favorite comments came from someone who shared how the three layers of truth felt different in the body and in time. "When I was in my Head," they said, "I was talking about the past—facts, résumé stuff. In my Heart, I was fully in the present. But when I dropped into the Core, that was the future. That's what I'm building toward."

Another person, reflecting on the Core round, said, "There was no shortage of what I want. It was all just there. Right on tap. But what struck me was the difference in energy—my Heart was meandering, full of emotions. But my Core was straight to the point."

Another participant—someone who'd just met their exercise partner an hour ago—said, "We started as strangers. But after three rounds we're not strangers anymore. We went deeper in ten minutes than I've gone in years."

That last comment is key.

You don't need hours or years to speak your truth and connect with someone. You can do it in just a few minutes. That's what Head-Heart-Core is all about.

USING HEAD-HEART-CORE: DECISION-MAKING

My recommendation is to start applying Head-Heart-Core in small ways, and build up to the bigger questions. A question like *"Where should I go on my next vacation?"* is fairly low stakes and doesn't force you to take any risky action. Start by laying out the Head truths—facts about your budget, your time frame, your schedule, and so on. Then explore your Heart truths. *What obligations do you feel currently that are determining what kind of vacation you need (e.g., big city or warm beach)? What emotions bubble up when you think about your desired getaway?* Finally, tap into your Core truths to learn what you really want to do.

Once you feel comfortable, try building up to bigger questions, like *"Should I take the next step in my romantic relationship?"* or *"Should I quit my job?"* Those require a bit more emotional energy and external shifts.

As you go through this exercise, don't hold back on being the complex and beautiful being you are. Be with whatever fears may come up for you as you both discover and express yourself authentically. In many cases, we feel fear because our truth may illuminate something that is out of alignment, and we fear having to make a change to get back into alignment.

If that resonates with you, I invite you to still do the exercise as fully and honestly as possible, and make a deal with yourself that you will not change anything in your external world—at least not right away. Knowing that action won't be required on the other side of this exercise might make it feel safer.

However, be prepared: Truth is one of those things that, once you see it, it's hard to unsee. And frankly, most people don't *want* to unsee their truth because it offers a tremendous sense of peace. To abandon truth is to step back into a place of anxiety. Once you are conscious of the misalignment and you know why you're anxious, it's not appealing to go back to that same situation.

USING HEAD-HEART-CORE: IN WORKSHOPS

I have led hundreds of people through this exercise in small groups and workshops. One of the most rewarding parts is witnessing the transformation that occurs when people engage with the

Head-Heart-Core framework. Time and again, participants tell me they've connected with others in ways they never thought possible. I often hear feedback like, "I've shared a cubicle with this colleague for ten years, but in three minutes, I felt closer to them than I ever have." These moments aren't just touching; they're a testament to how quickly and powerfully authenticity can foster connection.

To use this exercise in a group, start by pairing participants up. Then take turns going through the three steps using the same time limits you would in a solo exercise. Person A gets sixty seconds to share their Head truths, then Person B gets sixty seconds. Then both partners share their Heart truths for ninety seconds. Then both share their Core truths for sixty seconds. The only rule here is that each partner should fully listen to what the other person is saying— no rehearsing for your turn!

The simplicity of this framework is what makes it so effective. It doesn't require hours of deep discussion or exhausting emotional labor. In fact, I've found it resonates deeply with introverts and those in highly technical fields, where direct and efficient communication is highly valued. It's amazing to see the shift in energy after just a short exercise—walls come down and genuine understanding emerges.

I've seen this framework help people clarify their thoughts in real time, overcome fears of public speaking, and even resolve long-standing interpersonal conflicts. The results are often immediate: more clarity, less tension, and a newfound confidence in their ability to express themselves. What excites me most is that these aren't just workshop moments. Once people learn the Head-Heart-Core framework, they can take it with them to build stronger relationships at home, at work, and in their communities.

For me, the most profound result is when participants discover the courage to show up as their authentic selves. Whether they're asking for a raise, reconnecting with a family member, or simply introducing themselves to someone new, they leave the workshop equipped with the tools to express their truths and create meaningful connections. That's the kind of ripple effect I live for.

USING HEAD-HEART-CORE: IN PUBLIC SPEAKING

One of my favorite applications of the Head-Heart-Core framework is teaching sixth graders at my kids' middle school to structure their "Passion Talks." Each year, the school invites students to choose a subject they're passionate about and present it TED-style to their classmates and teachers. It's an incredible opportunity for kids to explore what lights them up while practicing public speaking, and I love being invited to guide them through the process.

When I step into the cafeteria filled with hundreds of nine- and ten-year-olds, the energy is palpable—equal parts excitement and chaos. I only have thirty-five minutes to teach kids about authentic communication, but let me tell you: These kids really get it. The simplicity of the Head-Heart-Core framework resonates immediately, because most of these kids still haven't developed many filters for their truths.

I start by explaining the three truths, keeping the language straightforward: "The Head is about the facts—what is true about your passion. The Heart is about how it makes you feel. And the Core is about what you want others to know or do about it." After modeling the framework myself and with a teacher, I break the kids into small groups and ask each student to think about a passion they'd like to share. They use the framework to jot down a few sentences under each category.

For example, if a student loves soccer, they might write:

- Head: "Soccer is the most popular sport in the world, and I play on my school's team."
- Heart: "I feel happy and energized when I'm on the field with my teammates."
- Core: "I want more kids to try soccer because it's a fun way to make friends and stay active."

Once they've written their ideas, they practice presenting to their group. In these small, supportive settings, you can see a transformation take place. Kids who were too shy to speak up at the beginning start to come alive as they share their passion in a way that feels authentic and structured.

Using Head-Heart-Core is a powerful way to tap into your full range of truth and connect with your audience when speaking in public. A very simple version would be to structure a speech with an introduction, a conclusion, and sections on Head, Heart, and Core in between. It's not the most sophisticated structure, but it's very clear and direct, and not a bad place to start if you're new to public speaking.

In a more sophisticated kind of talk where you're sharing multiple stories, you'll want to apply the Head-Heart-Core framework to each story, at least in your planning process. It will help give your talk a more consistent flow and format, along with a sense of momentum and vision.

USING HEAD-HEART-CORE: AT WORK

Even if you're not planning on getting up onstage, there are still lots of times that we get called on to speak publicly or make our case at work. It's amazing how many people in bigger companies fear being called on in a meeting. I've had people reach out to me to say, "I don't want to give a speech, but I would love to be able to talk in front of my team without turning bright red and stumbling over every word. Especially when I don't have any warning that I'm going to be called on."

In this case, I recommend writing the words "Head-Heart-Core" on a sticky note to have on your computer screen (for a Zoom call) or your notepad (for an in-person meeting) as a reminder of how to quickly access your truth if you do get called on. You'll be surprised at how this simple reminder can help you organize your thoughts and stay clear and concise on the fly. And, of course, the more you practice, the easier it will get.

Another place to use the Head-Heart-Core framework at work is to make your case in a one-on-one situation. For example, getting buy-in for a project you're passionate about, or asking for a raise.

Let's take a closer look at that last example. When asking for a raise:

Start with the Head by laying out the objective, verifiable facts about your performance. Highlight specific achievements, such as successfully completing projects or taking on additional responsibilities, and tie these to your company's goals. For example, you might say, "Over the past year, I've consistently met or exceeded my quota and delivered measurable results by increasing sales by 13 percent."

Next, move to the Heart, where you share your feelings to build emotional resonance. You could say, "I feel proud of the work I've done and excited about my growth in this role, but I've also felt undervalued at times because my contributions aren't fully reflected in my current compensation."

Finally, speak your Core truth by making a specific and actionable request: "What I want moving forward is a 10 percent raise to reflect the value I bring to the team, as well as opportunities to take on more leadership responsibilities."

USING HEAD-HEART-CORE: HARD CONVERSATIONS

It was one of those moments when I realized we needed to talk. My teenage son, Miles, had been spending a lot of time on his phone lately. And to be honest, I had, too. The constant ping of notifications, the endless scrolling—it felt like both of us were getting sucked into separate digital worlds, and I was starting to worry about the effect it was having on our relationship.

I knew that lecturing him or setting strict rules would backfire, but we needed to have the conversation. I decided to use the Head-Heart-Core framework to share my truth with him.

Starting with the Head, I sat down next to my son on the couch while he was scrolling through his phone. "Hey, Miles," I said gently. "I've noticed that we've both been spending a lot of time on our screens lately. It's not just you—I'm doing it, too. I even checked my phone's usage stats, and it's kind of shocking. It's easy to lose track of time while scrolling."

Moving to the Heart, I said, "Honestly, I feel a little sad about it. I miss talking with you, without distractions. I feel like we're both here in the same house, but we're not really connecting as much as we used to. And that makes me worry that we're missing out on moments we can't get back. We only have a few more years before you go off to college, and I'm scared we're not making the most of that time."

Finally, I ended with the Core by telling him, "Here's what I really want, Miles. I want us to put down our phones and spend more quality time together. I want to go paddleboarding with you. I want you to teach me how to fly your drone. I want us to set some boundaries together on phone usage, for both of us. Like a no-screens time in the evening or planning one tech-free activity each week. What do you think?"

It's important to make sure the Head facts don't come off as accusatory, because it can cause the other person to put their guard up so that they can't hear the Heart and the Core. Remember, when having a hard interpersonal conversation, the Head truths aren't there to help you make your case—this isn't a debate. They're there to create context for your Heart feelings and Core desire. The sooner you drop into your Heart, the more the other person is going to relax and understand where you're coming from, rather than feeling like they need to defend themselves.

The Core portion can also trigger some defensiveness. Be careful to express your desires in a way that doesn't come off as a list of demands, but rather as an expression of the better world you want to create with that person. If I had told Miles, "I want you to only use your phone an hour a day," he probably would have pushed back. Saying "I want us to have fun together and try new things" invited him into a shared world with me, one that we could both buy into.

When having hard conversations, it's important to remember that you can control only how you share your truth—not how it is received. There may be people in your life who won't be able to hear your truth, no matter how eloquently you speak it. There may be people who are not safe to speak the truth to, for whatever reason. In those situations, be as authentic as you feel safe to be, and then release your expectations about how the conversation should go.

My only goal when I use Head-Heart-Core is to be in my own truth and to make sure that truth is kind to the other person. How it lands, what the other person does with it—all that is out of my control. The cool part is that the more you embrace this mindset of letting go of the outcome, the easier it gets to tap into truths that make a real impact on the person you're speaking with. The more you stop trying to control how other people react to you, the closer you get to your center of authenticity, and the more deeply—and quickly—you make connections with those around you. And that's a beautiful thing.

TAKEAWAYS

- Authentic communication doesn't need to be long-winded or overly polished. The Head-Heart-Core method helps you quickly access and articulate your truth—what you think, feel, and want—so you can show up clearly and powerfully in any situation. It's a simple but transformative tool for getting to the point without losing depth.

- Before diving into truth sharing, you need to check in with yourself about your capacity and willingness to be real. You don't have to share everything with everyone, but knowing your limits and honoring them can help you express your truth with integrity—even if it's just asking for a quiet ride from your Lyft driver.

- The Head-Heart-Core method taps into three key truths: factual (Head), emotional (Heart), and desire-based (Core). Understanding and expressing all three leads to clearer communication and deeper self-awareness.

  - **Head truths (facts)** ground your message and provide context for connection.

  - **Heart truths (feelings)** are vulnerable and powerful, and when you share how you truly feel, you invite others to do the same—creating faster, more genuine connections.

  - **Your Core truth (desire)** is what you really want, and expressing it gives direction to your communication. Naming your desires clearly can be liberating and magnetic, helping others understand how to support or align with you.

- Use a three-part exercise to tap into your truths: first the facts (Head), then the feelings (Heart), and finally the desires (Core). This process helps you get clarity fast—whether for a tough decision, a conversation, or self-reflection—and sets you up to communicate from a place of alignment.

- You can use this framework in decision-making, in workshops, in public speaking, at work, and in having hard conversations. Ultimately, Head-Heart-Core creates a balanced, compassionate way to share your truth. You can't control how others respond, but you *can* speak from a place of clarity and kindness.

PART II

DISCOVER YOUR PURPOSE

CHAPTER 4

TELL YOUR STORY

It's time to get down to the business of the Dig.

The goal of the Dig is simple: to unearth your purpose and give it words so you can express it to other people. I believe that every human is here for a reason. The problem is that if our reason feels too murky and complicated, our message stays locked inside us and doesn't create the connections we're meant to make in this world.

Through the Dig, we'll refine your purpose into just one word. But the point of the Dig isn't to simplify the beautiful, messy complexity that is every human being—it's to create a space that honors your story and unique truths, then to help you focus and clarify it in a way that empowers you to act, lead, share, and *live*.

The next few chapters will lead you through each step of the Dig, beginning with your story and ending by creating a set of tools that will help you embrace your truth and express it to the world.

Here's what we're going to do:

Step 1: Tell Your Story. First, start by telling your life story from birth to the present day. Think of all the things you've lived through as data we are mining. Then analyze your story to uncover patterns and themes that keep recurring in your life, and summarize each of them in just one word.

Step 2: Discover Your Human Operating System. Next, we'll pare those recurring one-word themes we unearthed down to ten or fewer, using the Resonance Meter to identify the most powerful ones for you. These words work together in a unique shape and flow to reveal your human operating system.

Step 3: Uncover Your Dig Word. Buried among the words in your operating system is just one word—your *why*. It's both your superpower and your Achilles' heel, and we'll sift through your operating system to find it. (And align with it!)

Step 4: Integrate Your Results. Finally, we'll pull it all together and express it with words. I'll give you a set of tools to help keep you in tune with what you learned and stay aligned with your Dig word day in and day out.

Are you ready to claim your superpowers and shine a light that will illuminate your path forward? The world is waiting for your truth! And it begins with your story.

SEEING THE WHOLE YOU

I've known Rosalind Wiseman for many years. She is a longtime friend, a fierce advocate for young people, and the author of *Queen Bees and Wannabes*, the book that inspired the movie *Mean Girls*. I knew Rosalind's story well before our Dig sessions—both her public narrative of success and struggle, and the moments that she shared with me in private as friends. But listening to her systematically go through the events of her life taught me something new about her.

Rosalind's stories were complex and nuanced. After she shared about her childhood navigating the elite social circles of Washington, DC, we went on to talk about the rude awakenings of a young woman at college and what she'd learned in her early career working with teens. We touched on the massive success of *Queen Bees and Wannabes*, as well as the challenges that came with that kind of spotlight. We talked about her decision to go public about her negative experience with Tina Fey and Paramount (after being denied any profits from the *Mean Girls* theatrical production and movie) and her decision to share what it's like to have people with more power use it against you. She ultimately didn't win anything beyond speaking out, but she still believes it was worth doing.

The anecdotes Rosalind shared might have seemed scattered out of context, but together they formed a clear pattern—like mosaic tiles that create a picture when you step back to view them as a whole.

Her life was full of moments where she stood up for others and challenged broken systems that didn't value the humans within them. She'd seen how power could be weaponized, and she rebelled against showing respect to those who hadn't earned it, while protesting social hierarchies that seemed designed to strip people of their dignity. Over and over again, Rosalind was the one who said, "No. Everyone deserves to be treated with dignity."

Long before the book, the movie, or the media spotlight, Rosalind was already on a lifelong journey to understand "worth."

As she put it so beautifully in her 2025 commencement speech at Occidental College: "When we compete to demand respect, it becomes a race to the bottom. But when we compete to demand dignity, it becomes a race to the top." That concept is "worth" in action. It reflects her active, defiant belief in the value of every human being—and her drive to help others understand it, too.

When we drilled down through her stories, it became clear that her work and her writing are all in service of reminding people of their value. She doesn't just want people to be treated better—she wants systems to be restructured so that dignity is baked in from the start.

No matter the story, knowing her worth and helping others understand theirs was the theme.

The first step of finding those patterns in your own life is to record your story, starting from the very beginning and hitting all the major points of your life through the present day. This process can be deeply cathartic. In almost every one of the Digs I do, my client experiences a deep sense of release when they realize they have permission to tell their story, unfiltered and uninterrupted.

Once you begin this exercise, it might feel like a floodgate of words and memories is opening up within you. But it's also okay to feel nervous, especially if you have traumatic events in your past, or you're holding shame about certain parts of your story. If that's the case, I invite you to approach this process with curiosity rather than worry. The nice thing about doing a solo Dig—meaning without a facilitator to guide you—is that you have complete privacy to explore without worrying about anyone else's opinion. Embrace the freedom to say or write whatever you like, without censorship. No one will ever listen to your recordings or read your writings (though you might come back to this exercise to mine your story for content later, if you like).

This isn't a creative writing exercise, so you can go ahead and stop stressing if that's not your jam! You don't have to worry about grammar, or proper word use, or whether or not you're using commas correctly. You don't even have to worry about complete sentences. Right now, all you're doing is making sure that your story lives outside yourself so you can observe it with some level of objectivity.

You might be thinking, *I already know my story. Why do I need to tell it to myself?* Well, most of the stories we carry about our lives are filtered through layers of habit, assumption, and emotion. By going through your life story in a chronological way and speaking these stories out loud (or writing them down), you take those stories out of the realm of the abstract and create something you can hold up to the light and see in new ways.

And, just like when I finally heard my dear friend Rosalind's story told from start to finish, you'll find that clear patterns will emerge.

TELL YOUR STORY

To complete this exercise, you'll need only three tools:

1. A pen or pencil (that's right, we're going analog!)
2. A pad of sticky notes
3. Your phone (or recording device)

Using the voice memo app on your phone, and guided by the questions in the next section, start narrating your life story in chronological order. (If you like to write, you're welcome to free-write, so long as you're sure you can do it without editorializing or getting caught up in making pretty prose; this needs to be fast and raw.)

While all of us have many chapters in our lives, for efficiency's sake you're going to break your life down into three parts: Childhood, Adulthood, and Present Day. Set your timer for ten-minute increments—one for each part. If it takes a little more time for you to feel like you've gotten your whole story out, that's fine, but don't spend too much time here. You don't want to get overwhelmed. You do, however, want to share enough stories and feelings to give you plenty of data to work with later.

The reason we break the chapters of our lives into three parts is to help us spot patterns that have remained consistent in our lives. My theory is that our human operating systems (and Dig words) don't change as we age. I'll explain operating systems more fully in the next chapter, but for now just know that the human operating system is made up of the core parts of our identity that drove us as children—and still drive us as adults. Finding commonalities in our stories from each stage of life helps us identify those core parts.

In childhood, each of us was given stories to help us navigate our truth or learn about our purpose. Some of us experienced childhoods where we were totally in the frequency of our operating systems, which allowed us to steep in that frequency and master it. Some of us experienced childhoods that were at odds with our operating systems, giving us the opportunity to clarify our frequency through the places we felt out of alignment with the world around us.

For example, look at my client Anthony Trucks, whom I mentioned in the introduction. Anthony's Dig word is "Lift." As a kid, Anthony was told he wouldn't amount to anything. He was bounced between foster homes, faced racial barriers, and had to fight for every opportunity. But instead of letting that define him, he used it as fuel. Every challenge became another chance for him to prove himself and fight for better and better opportunities. So when Anthony finally realized his childhood dream of making it to the NFL, it felt like he couldn't possibly fly any higher—until, within two months, a shoulder injury sent him crashing back down. He found himself working as a personal trainer at a gym to support his family.

Anthony could have let that setback drag him down for good. Instead, he used it as an opportunity to pivot and open his own gym and become his own boss. What struck me as I listened to the ups and downs of Anthony's early life, his NFL dreams, his rocky entrepreneurial ventures, his struggling marriage, was his constant drive to lift himself and those around him. Because Anthony had realized that his purpose wasn't just to create his own success. He wanted to help others do the same.

Now Anthony uses his platform to help people lift themselves up, whether it's in business, athletics, or personal development. He speaks, he coaches, he mentors, and he embodies the very thing he needed most when he was younger—someone to believe that rising above your circumstances is possible.

Our stories—both good and bad—show us what we value and how we act under pressure. What causes us to thrive, and what causes us to lose our way. Our stories of success and joy show us places where we are living in our full truth. Our stories of hardship and pain illuminate the experiences we needed to have in order to come through to the other side with lessons for our future selves.

DEALING WITH HARD STORIES

Talking about our stories in the context of a Dig can be wildly therapeutic, but it can also bring up a whole bunch of stuff you might not be prepared to deal with. If you don't want to touch specific stories, that's fine. You don't have to go anywhere you don't want to during this exercise—I promise you'll still be able to find your human operating system and Dig word, even if there are specific places you don't feel like bringing to light at this moment.

Over the years, a few clients have flat-out refused to share stories from certain chapters in their lives with me during our Dig. Maybe they didn't want to talk about their childhood, or a specific relationship or job was off-limits. I never pressed them, because the cool thing about the Dig is that you can spot patterns without knowing every single detail. As long as you gather data from enough parts of your life to start picking out themes, you're good.

In this process, I encourage you to trust yourself. If it doesn't feel right to resurface certain things, don't do it. There's no pressure. It's not necessary. On the flip side, things might bubble up in this process that you really *do* want to explore. Certain stories might feel irrelevant in the moment, or like non sequiturs, but you're still really compelled by them. You might think, *Why the hell would I say this?* Say it anyway. Trust your instincts and honor what comes up as important, even if it doesn't make logical sense at the time.

Get out of your own way and let your intuition guide you.

Ultimately, this mining process is about gathering the raw material of your life—the moments, experiences, and emotions that have shaped you. By bringing these stories into the light, you will begin to see them for what they are: not just scattered pieces of a chaotic past but a rich, textured map of who you are and where you've been. And from this map, we can begin to uncover the Core truths that resonate most deeply with your purpose and your authentic self.

The truth is not always super comfortable. Sometimes, once you see it, you can't unsee it. But the reward is greater alignment with your authentic self.

GUIDING QUESTIONS

As you work your way through the story of your life, your goal will be to capture the facts of your life and your feelings about those facts, both good and not so good. In fact, the stronger the emotion in either direction, the more important it will be that you express it. Those feelings are important clues to the essence of you.

Don't worry about analyzing anything during this part of the exercise—we'll do that afterward. If you get stuck anywhere in your story, or find yourself wandering off track, a good all-purpose question to get you back on track is: *"So, what happened next?"*

Childhood (10 minutes)

- What's your birthday; where were you born?

- Do you have any siblings—how are you like and/or different from them?

- How would you describe your parents?

- How would you describe yourself as a child?

- How would the person closest to you in your family describe you as a child?

- When you look back on childhood, how do you feel about it?

- What's your best childhood memory? The worst?

- What was the hardest part about growing up?

- What were the main takeaways from that experience?

Adulthood (10 minutes)

- Did you go to college? If so, what did you major in and why?

- Did you travel? Where? Why?

- What was your first job? What jobs did you take after that? What did you like and dislike about each of these?

- Where have you lived? What pulled you there?

- What was your romantic life like? Did you choose partnership or marriage?

- Did you get divorced? Why did you or your partner choose to leave?

- Did you experience any significant health challenges?

- Did you experience any significant losses?

- Did you experience any significant triumphs or joys?

Present Day (10 minutes)

- What would the people closest to you say are your super-powers?

- What would the people closest to you say you struggle with the most?

- Think of a recent event that really pissed you off. Why did it anger you so much?

- Think of a recent event that made you feel hurt. Why was it so painful?

- Think of a recent event where you experienced joy. Why did it make you so happy?

- What little things irritate you, and why?

- What are some of your favorite phrases? For instance, "Seize the day!" or "Anyone can change the world!" or "No matter what, take care of your people!" or "Be true to yourself!"

- If you could do anything, what would you do?

- What's the hardest thing you've ever been through?

- Imagine you're on your deathbed and there's not much time left. What advice or life wisdom do you leave behind for the people you love most?*

- In seven words or less, what advice would you give your twenty-two-year-old self?*

- What are your nonnegotiables or deal breakers with regard to relationships and work?*

    (* Don't skip these last questions! They squeeze the juice out of who we really are.)

EXAMINING YOUR STORIES FOR THEMES

Once you're done sharing your story, it's time to start analyzing it in search of patterns and themes. During a facilitated Dig, the facilitator will be doing some of this work behind the scenes while they listen to your story. But when Digging yourself (I call this a solo Dig), you'll break this work into two parts because it's impossible to express and analyze at the same time.

Grab your sticky notes—it's time to start pulling out themes! The number of sticky notes you'll have at the end of this exercise will vary. You'll know you're done when you feel a sense of completion. Some people wind up with fifty sticky notes; some will have fewer. Either way is fine. Don't overthink this step, but do try to come up with a minimum of twenty words (you'll need this many to make sure you have enough to work with when you move to the next step in the Dig).

1. Distill Your Story

Start by reviewing your story. If you did a voice recording, either type out a transcript (if you find that satisfying) or use any free online transcription service to get your words in print. Then grab your stack of sticky notes and start summarizing! Think about this step as condensing your thoughts and feelings into their most succinct yet expressive form.

Using one color sticky note, write down a five- or six-word summary of every major moment of your life and arrange them sequentially on a table or wall in front of you.

For example:

- Was eldest of three
- Grew up moving around a lot
- Went to college in Iowa

You might also write down anything profound that leaps out at you while you're summarizing your story, for example, phrases that resonate as a fundamental belief, such as "Leave things better than how you found them" or "Family is everything."

Note that these kinds of thoughts don't necessarily have any inherent negative or positive value. They simply represent a frequency. "Family is everything" could mean something completely different when spoken by someone who came from a loving, intact family and when spoken by someone who felt abandoned and betrayed by theirs.

The table or wall is a story spread, with sticky notes for major points and ideas. You'll notice there's a bit of meandering—that's absolutely okay. Don't edit yourself here, just jot down everything that jumps out to you.

2. Identify Themes

Once you have your complex and beautiful life distilled into a grid of sticky notes, look over the expanse of your life stories. Frequently you'll notice that you repeat a word over and over again, such as "possible," "soul," "adventure," or "faith." Or you might just start noticing patterns that can be summed up in a single word, even if you didn't specifically use that word.

For example, you might realize that whether it was stray animals, parents, friends, or coworkers, you've always felt compelled to take care of others when they're suffering. So you might write down the word "care" or "nurture," depending on which resonates most

Traveled overseas after college	Met waiter from New York who loved his job	Waiting tables and traveling for a decade	Met spouse, didn't believe they really wanted to travel, pleasantly surprised	Went to South America together for 6 months after wedding
I love the feeling of getting in the car and going	Feels like there's nothing to come back to	Why not keep driving?	Tension of working day job and passion	Always wanted to get away from high school
Came back from South America with $50, went back to waiting tables	Stress dreams about being a server	Decided to pursue "real career"	Got a real day job	Hated having a desk job 9–5
Quit, strung together a few freelance jobs, loved the flexibility	Moved to a different town for spouse's job, settled into routine	Never had kids, I didn't want them, always knew that since high school, kids tie you down	Had friends who got pregnant in high school, slammed door on their possibilities	Love my nieces and nephews, love spoiling them

strongly. Remember, there's no right or wrong answer here. Lean into your Resonance Meter, and trust that your truth will make itself known if you stay open to it.

As you identify any recurring themes and words, write each of them down on their own sticky note. (You can use a different color for these notes if you like.) Avoid writing descriptor words. The goal isn't to write down your attributes or your flaws, which have positive and negative connotations and therefore carry a judgment. You're not labeling yourself—you're naming your *responses* to various events in your life, and the patterns that reveal themselves. What you're looking for is truth, which is inherently neutral.

Don't stress too much about all this, though. The word you write is actually less important than the vibe—the frequency—of the word. If it feels right, it's right.

Taking a look at the example on page 103, here are some words that might come out of it.

- Freedom
- Go
- Momentum
- Possibility
- Delight
- Choose

3. Identify Superpowers, Struggles, and Nonnegotiables

As you start unearthing patterns and themes, be on the lookout for three key things, and jot them down on their own color of sticky note. (Here's a hint: You'll probably find those answers by asking the questions marked with an asterisk.)

Your superpowers: instances where you really shine and find joy, and where things come easily to you. Notice moments in your life when you were really in the flow, times you had breakthroughs in your life and career, and times you felt truly aligned.

Your struggles: where you tend to get stuck and things don't come easy. Notice patterns in the ways you tend to get in your own way, or similarities in the kinds of obstacles you have encountered throughout your life.

Your nonnegotiables: those beliefs and values that are fundamental pillars in your worldview. Notice strong feelings that feel like Core truths, and ask yourself why you reacted that way, whether in the moment or now, in the retelling. These are usually short, direct statements.

Back to the story spread, you can start to pull out some foundational patterns even in these few sticky notes.

- Superpowers: flexibility, exploration
- Struggles: needing to feel free, choosing what to do, office life
- Nonnegotiables: freedom is critical

TOOLS FOR DIGGING DEEPER

Sometimes, patterns and themes might immediately become clear. Other times, it might be more of a struggle to uncover our deeper reasons and motivations. Why do certain moments stick with us? Why do some memories feel heavy while others feel light? Why do we keep telling ourselves the same stories over and over?

If you're feeling stuck, try some of these tools to help you Dig deeper.

The 5 Whys

One of the simplest and most powerful tools I use to help people Dig deeper is the 5 Whys method. I didn't create this technique—it's a problem-solving framework devised by Japanese inventor (and founder of Toyota) Sakichi Toyoda and is often used in coaching and business—but I've found it incredibly useful in personal growth work as well.[1] The idea is straightforward: Start with a belief or statement about yourself, and then ask "Why?" five times. Each time, push yourself to Dig deeper.

For example, let's say you tell yourself, "I've always had to work harder than everyone else."

1. Why is that? *Because I feel like I have something to prove.*
2. Why do I feel like I have something to prove? *Because I grew up in a family where success was expected.*
3. Why was success so important in my family? *Because failure was seen as weakness.*
4. Why was failure seen as weakness? *Because my parents were afraid of losing control.*
5. Why does that matter to you now? *Because I've been living my life trying to avoid failure instead of pursuing what truly matters to me.*

Or, to take another example: "I have a hard time expressing my emotions to others, so I try to stay stoic."

1. Why is that? *Because when I express my emotions, I feel like I can't take care of myself.*
2. Why do I feel that way? *Because I associate being stoic with being strong and capable.*
3. Why do I believe that? *Because whenever I was upset as a child, my parents told me to keep my chin up and be strong.*
4. Why did my parents equate strength with stoicism? *Because that's the lesson they learned from their parents.*

5. Why did my grandparents believe that? *Because they were refugees from a war in their country and learned to shut their emotions down to survive.*

By the end of this process, you've moved from a general belief to something much deeper. You've realized that your drive to work hard might not be about passion but rather about fear. You've learned that your hesitance around expressing emotions is a trauma response that served your grandparents but doesn't serve you. And once you see that, you can begin noticing deeper patterns.

Challenge Your Assumptions

Another way to Dig deeper is to challenge your own assumptions. One of the hardest parts of doing a solo Dig is that we don't always notice when we're making assumptions about our own stories. We rarely question the stories we tell ourselves about our past, but what if, instead of assuming we already understand everything about who we are, we approached our own experiences with curiosity?

As you review your stories, try to put yourself in the shoes of a stranger and ask questions whose answers might seem obvious to you. When you find yourself making matter-of-fact statements or glossing over things that seem business as usual to you, imagine having to explain that thing to an outsider.

The beauty of solo Digging, though, is that you can drop all the filters you might normally have when talking about your life to an outsider. No one is watching, not even a trained facilitator. You can be bolder than you normally would. You can be louder and more irreverent; you can be edgier; you can be more raw.

Here are some questions to help you challenge your assumptions about a story:

- What does this story say about me?
- Why do I tell this story the way I do?
- What emotions did I feel in that moment?
- What beliefs about myself or the world shaped my choices?
- If I were hearing this story from someone else, what questions would I ask them?

Approach this process with the same openness and curiosity you'd bring to a conversation with a close friend. Even the most well-worn stories can reveal something new if you're willing to look closer.

Note Your Resistance

Elizabeth Durham and I go way back—we were sorority sisters in college, and we connected once more after she moved to Colorado with her husband and five kids. When we reconnected, Elizabeth's world had been turned upside down. Both she and several of her children have severe food allergies, which made something as simple as going out to eat nearly impossible. So, in true Elizabeth fashion, she rolled up her sleeves, taught herself how to bake allergy-safe treats, and launched a bakery in Colorado Springs called Sweet Elizabeth's.

It quickly gathered a cult following of families who have food allergies—a group that can often feel isolated and exhausted. Her bakery gathered loyal customers because she created a place where families feel seen, safe, and understood. (Oh, and because her treats are delicious!) Yet, despite her public persona and educational social media presence, she's often struggled with being seen herself.

When Elizabeth and I did her Dig, she was already teetering on the edge of burnout—again. She's the kind of person who gives and gives and who enjoys educating and empowering others. But being in the spotlight takes so much out of her, especially because her own autoimmune disorder means that she has to protect her own energy fiercely. Over and over, she told stories of pouring so much of her own light into the world that she had completely depleted her own batteries. It was a clear pattern.

We were doing her Dig in a conference room with a small group, and I remember the moment her Dig word landed. We'd been circling around words like "heal" and "educate"—words that felt safer, more aligned with her role as a baker, a mom, an advocate. But when we landed on "Shine," deep emotions bubbled to the surface.

Elizabeth didn't want "Shine" to be her purpose, and yet our purpose isn't something any of us get to choose. She was *already* a brilliant light for her family. She was *already* a beacon of hope for those with severe food allergies. She was *already* a bright star in her business community. But for Elizabeth, it's never been about being in the spotlight. And it was clear from her stories that she'd spent too many cycles shining brightly and burning out. "Shine" embodies her superpower, but it's also her greatest challenge.

She's still learning what it means to live into that word, to honor her truth without depleting her reserves. But that's part of the beauty of the Dig.

I don't want you to worry about finding your Dig word yet—that's still a few chapters away. But I *do* want you to pay attention to the words that make you cringe a little. They're often the ones that speak most deeply to our Core truth.

Sometimes you might note resistance around a certain thought, idea, or story. Here's the thing: Resistance is a sign that something important is hiding beneath the surface, and you might just need to take a step back in order to let it bubble up. Resistance isn't a stop sign—it's an invitation. When you feel yourself shutting down, pulling back, or being dismissive, here's how to move through it:

- Acknowledge the resistance. Instead of judging yourself for it, get curious. What's coming up for you? What part of your story feels hard to face? Name it so you can claim it.
- Take the pressure off. You don't have to get everything "right" in one sitting. If something feels too heavy, move to another part of your story and come back later.
- Let yourself sit with the discomfort. Clarity doesn't always come in bright, blazing flashes of light. Give yourself time to process and to let things reveal themselves slowly.
- Trust that whatever comes up is exactly what needs to. Even if you don't fully understand why a memory or emotion is surfacing, trust that it's showing up for a reason.

If you hit resistance, don't panic. Don't force it. Just stay open. Stay curious. Go for a walk, if necessary. And most of all, be honest with yourself. Because the deeper you go, the closer you get to the core of who you are—and that's where real transformation begins.

TAKEAWAYS

- The first step of the Dig is to record your life story—quickly, honestly, and without self-editing. By dividing your life into three stages (Childhood, Adulthood, Present Day), you'll begin to notice recurring themes and emotional patterns. This step isn't about perfect storytelling—it's about capturing raw data for reflection.
- Use the questions in this chapter to guide you, and follow your instincts. If a certain chapter of your life feels too painful to dive into, it's okay to leave it be (or reach out to a licensed mental health professional to talk through it). If a certain story or thought captures

your attention, keep exploring—even if it feels irrelevant. Strong emotional responses signal important clues to your deeper truths.

- Once you've told your story, the next step is analysis. Using sticky notes, distill major life moments into succinct summaries and identify recurring themes and values. This pattern recognition lays the foundation for discovering your human operating system and Dig word.

- While sorting through your themes, look for moments that highlight your strengths, consistent challenges, and core values. These superpowers, struggles, and nonnegotiables are core elements that help you understand your internal wiring—what energizes you, what drains you, and what you'll never compromise on.

- If you get stuck, several tools can help you uncover deeper meaning:
    - **Know Your Whys:** Keep asking "Why?" to dive below your surface beliefs and uncover deeper fears and motivations.
    - **Challenge Your Assumptions:** Approach familiar stories with fresh curiosity.
    - **Note Your Resistance:** Understand that discomfort is a signal of something meaningful just beneath the surface. Trust that even difficult memories hold insight.

CHAPTER 5

REMEMBER YOUR HUMAN OPERATING SYSTEM

When Erica started telling me about her wedding during her Dig, I could tell something was off. She was an introvert who was very much in love with her fiancé—who was also an introvert. Erica was managing the logistics and planning just fine. But her energy felt low, like she was preparing for a celebration she didn't actually want.

The issue revealed itself as we began to Dig. It was brimming with words that reflected her need for intimacy and deep connection and showed how much she required space and time for reflection in order to fully show up and be present. The idea of a big, busy wedding was grating against her core being, but she felt like that's what was expected of her.

Her operating system had unearthed the word "good," so I asked her a simple question: When it came to her wedding, what would feel good to her?

For Erica, "good" meant intimate. It meant candlelight. It meant a day filled with quiet moments, deep connection with a few friends, and a space where she and her fiancé could be fully present without feeling overwhelmed. A big, traditional wedding didn't feel good to her. Standing in front of a hundred people, reciting personal vows into a microphone? That felt downright terrible.

As soon as she started describing her ideal wedding, her entire frequency changed. She lit up. It was as if, for the first time, she realized that she could design a wedding that actually felt like her. But then the fear crept back in. "Can we really do that?" she asked.

Erica had been planning a wedding that centered around the expectations of her friends, family, and society—but it didn't align with her operating system. A wedding should be a joyful occasion, but for Erica, it was beginning to feel more like an obligation. She'd been feeling that way long before her Dig, but when I helped her remember her operating system, she was finally able to put a finger on why.

Most of us spend our lives trying to fit into expectations—of our families, our workplaces, society at large. We absorb unspoken rules about who we're supposed to be, how we should behave, and what success looks like. But those rules and expectations don't always align with who we are at our core, leaving us feeling off-kilter in ways that are sometimes subtle and sometimes extremely glaring. And if we never take the time to understand how we really operate, we may go our whole lives not knowing how to fix it when things feel off.

Your human operating system is not something you choose. It's the way you naturally process the world, the patterns that emerge over and over in your life. Remembering your operating system is a daily invitation to make choices in alignment with who you really are. It's permission to say no to things that drain you and yes to what lights you up. It's the freedom to stop justifying yourself—to stand firmly in your truth, without feeling like you have to explain or defend it.

Buoyed by radical self-permission and her newfound understanding of how she operated at her core, Erica started asking herself what would feel good in her wedding. She followed her internal compass toward exactly what she needed to feel aligned and at peace. She and her fiancé redesigned the entire experience to feel more intimate, building in quiet moments and shifting traditions to align with their personalities.

The result? A wedding that didn't just meet expectations but felt absolutely perfect to Erica, her husband, and everyone who knew them.

WHAT IS A HUMAN OPERATING SYSTEM?

In technological terms, an operating system refers to the controlling program on your computer, phone, or other device that manages the rest of the hardware and software. (Think Windows, macOS, or Linux.) Without an OS installed, none of your other programs or apps will run.

For people, a human operating system (HOS) serves the same controlling function. It's the metaphorical framework made up of your core values, guiding principles, and everything else that contributes to your unique way of functioning in the world. Whether or not you've ever thought about it in those terms, your operating system has been humming away in the background your entire life, subtly directing your responses, reactions, and deepest motivations to shape the way you approach challenges, relationships, and decisions.

Our operating system isn't about the *thing* we do; it's about *how* we do it. When our circumstances or environment allows our operating system to function smoothly and express itself, we feel good, we're productive, and we achieve success (however we define it).

When we're in situations that don't mesh with our operating system, we stall out. We're irritable. We find it hard to make progress or communicate.

You can use your HOS as a dual-purpose tool. On one hand, it allows you to see your repeating patterns and identify when they work for you and under what circumstances they don't. On the other, once you're aware of these patterns, you can choose to respond differently. The HOS can be a guide that helps you confidently shape your future the next time you need to make a decision.

An easy way to see how this plays out is by looking at how we make clothing or home goods purchases. For many of us, these kinds of purchases are intimately tied to our identities. We like what we like, even if we can't always explain why. I fell unreasonably in love with a pair of sneakers not long ago. As soon as I put them on, I loved them. When I tried to articulate the reason, I realized it's because they're classy and a little weird, which is how I like to think of myself. When I put those sneakers on, I felt like me. I felt like I could wear them to almost any occasion and authentically express myself in them, and I wouldn't feel that way if I were to wear something like a classic pair of pumps.

For another example, let's say you just bought a new couch. You'd always imagined something soft, plush, curvy, and white, but you have young kids and three dogs. So, instead, you made a practical choice and bought a solid, scratch-resistant, dark-colored couch. It was the smart move, right? The only problem is that now, every time you really stop and look at your new piece of furniture, you feel a twinge of regret. Why?

It could be because your operating system revolves around beauty, design, harmony, and bringing out the best in everyone. This couch isn't awful, but it's not what you'd call a beautiful piece of design. It doesn't feel harmonious, and it definitely doesn't pull the room together. What's done is done, though. You had good reasons for making the choice you did, and eventually you get used to the couch. You dress it up with some fun pillows and it looks perfectly nice, serves its purpose, and reveals no stains or wear through years of heavy use. All good, right?

Then one day, after your kids are grown and your dogs are too old to jump on the couch, you decide it's finally time to replace the old stalwart and buy the couch you always wanted. The day it's delivered, you drop onto your soft, plushy white cushions and lean your head back. A smile touches your lips, and you sigh contentedly.

You *love* this couch.

You never want to leave it. And from then on, you find that your entire daily routine has shifted. Now you take your morning coffee curled up on the couch and spend your evenings reading in this comfortable, harmonious room—instead of scrolling on your phone in your bedroom. This room is furnished exactly the way you wanted it, and you can feel the perfection in your soul.

That's what alignment feels like.

Now, imagine if instead of shoes or a couch, we were talking about a job, a relationship, a school, or a volunteer project. Maybe you've always been drawn to work with animals, but you chose a "safe" career path in accounting and now you dread going to work every morning. Maybe you married a partner who doesn't like change, while your operating system thrives on a diet of fresh, new experiences, and every day you feel more disconnected from the person you're supposed to spend the rest of your life with.

These types of decisions are so much more impactful than an impulse shopping purchase. Spending a decade with a couch you aren't in love with isn't that big a deal in the grand scheme of things.

But the consequences of choosing a job or relationship or making another long-term decision that's out of alignment with your operating system is actively harmful. Even if (*especially* if) you pretend everything is just fine.

Living out of alignment with your operating system is a constant, massive drain on your battery. It's like paddling upstream—not only are you wearing yourself out by working against the current; you're missing out on the opportunity to harness the river's flow in order to make massive leaps and bounds in your life.

Imagine how you could thrive if you were working *with* your operating system instead of against it!

That's why understanding your operating system is so valuable. When you're aware of your HOS, when you acknowledge it, and when you consciously make choices that align with it as much as possible, it leaves you functioning at full power all the time. You can be more deliberate about seeking out situations where you'll thrive, and you can more easily troubleshoot what's going on when you feel stalled out. In other words, understanding your operating system gives you a reliable funnel for deciding what you're going to add to or remove from your life.

That, my friend, is the secret to an enjoyable, fulfilling, and successful career and life.

This isn't to say that you'll always be able to refuse to engage with people or opportunities that don't align with your HOS; sometimes you do what you gotta do—and we'll talk about that in part 3. But it's incredibly helpful to be aware of when you're in (or out of) alignment. The better you understand your operating system, the easier it is for you to figure out why things are or aren't working the way you'd like them to, where you belong, or where you'd like to go.

EVERYONE'S HUMAN
OPERATING SYSTEM IS UNIQUE

Erica hadn't come to work with me specifically because of her wedding, but a wedding is exactly what brought Nick to one of my workshops. He'd been asked to give the best man speech at his friend's wedding, and he didn't want to mess up this important opportunity—which is very admirable. Sometimes we underestimate those pivotal life moments of having people's undivided attention and brush them off as not that important. But not Nick.

He joined a group workshop I was teaching, along with others who had a speech to prepare. I started the group off by going through a modified version of the Dig, because by that point in my speech consulting career I'd learned the value of helping them find that one word that was the heartbeat of *why* they wanted to give this talk, and *what* they wanted to infuse into their message.

When Nick showed up to the workshop, he was a corporate guy. Even in the few hours we had together at the workshop, I could tell he didn't jibe with his job. When he talked about it, his energy was low and suppressed. It was clear he felt constrained at work and knew he could bring more to the world. As he told his story and shared what drove him and lit him up, it became clear to me.

This man is here to have a good time.

His operating system revolved around having fun, and when we pinpointed that and worked it into his speech, it all came alive. He gave that wedding speech and was the life of the party, just like he loved to be. Afterward, he sent me a happy text saying how much joy the speech brought to him and everyone in the room.

While I didn't say it out loud at the time, I was certainly thinking, *This guy is never gonna last in the corporate world*. Having fun is absolutely critical to Nick's operating system. Not to say corporate jobs can't ever be fun—but someone whose life purpose is to truly live in a frequency of joy, pleasure, and laughter is going to have a hard time accessing that frequency consistently in a corporate job.

So I wasn't that surprised when I heard Nick left his corporate job soon after that speech workshop. Instead, he decided to start a cocktail mixer company called Strongwater.

Here's a short version of the Strongwater story: "Strongwater is inspired by the strongwater shops of old, which hawked elixirs as medicine. Our earliest bitters followed that tradition, drawing on the healing powers and powerful flavors of botanicals as modern-day potions.... Today, we're shifting closer to our roots, imagining whole-plant beverages with functional benefits and flavors that transport you to different places, moods, and memories."

Talk about making "being the life of the party" your full-time job!

I've done more than a thousand Digs, and I can say that it's rare for someone's operating system to change. On a few occasions their words have shifted, but overall the HOS that makes us tick today is the same one that's propelled us since we were five years old. How we dealt with our fourth-grade teacher is probably how we deal with our boss or our partner today—and how we'll deal with anyone we meet in the future.

This doesn't mean we're stuck forever in our patterns, of course. I'm not saying you have to stay trapped in old stories or harmful habits. As we age, rack up new experiences, and meet new people, our core values and priorities can change. We can put in the work to shift our mindsets, address the wounding messages we heard as children, and overcome our traumas.

Through it all, though, our HOS tends to stay the same.

Sometimes people worry that means they'll be locked into one way of being or living. Will they ever be able to settle down with a life partner if their operating system drives them to keep their possibilities open? Will they ever learn how to take the leaps they want to in business if their operating system values safety and security?

I have good news! Your human operating system doesn't lock you into a single definition of happiness. Just because you value keeping possibilities open doesn't mean you can't find happiness in the possibility of a long-term partner. Just because you value safety doesn't mean you can't find that safety through taking risks to grow your business.

It's not always *what* you do for a living, but *how* you do it. In Nick's case, having fun meant creating a product that inspired people to share their own good times with others. Anyone who's ever been an entrepreneur can tell you that being your own boss isn't always fun—but Nick was able to create the playful, uplifting environment his operating system thrives in.

Our operating systems offer us guidance but never rules, suggestions but never judgment. I've learned over the years that we can infuse our frequencies in almost any setting, even ones that are immensely challenging. And yet, there's also something to be said for removing obstacles so that we can live more in flow with our natural frequencies.

For example, my operating system can be summed up with the statement "I need to find my frequency, be free to authentically express myself, to align with my purpose and create and connect with integrity and grace, so that everyone can soar." Throughout my life, I have and will forever filter my experiences through the lens of freedom to authentically express myself. Do I have it? Do others have it? Can they achieve it? Can I help them achieve it?

With words like "free" and "authentic" in my operating system, it makes sense that I find joy and fulfillment being an entrepreneur. But that doesn't mean that being an entrepreneur is the only career path that could make me happy. I could be very successful at a corporate job so long as I felt free within it to authentically express myself and that it was a purpose-driven venture. It's not the specific situation that defines freedom (and therefore my happiness)—it's the *frequency* of the situation. And, remember, the Dig is all about understanding these frequencies so that we can work with them instead of fighting against them.

There's plenty of room for self-improvement and growth, even as we accept that we're each a little more consistent and predictable than we thought. At the same time, it's my hope that this realization eases any pressure you might feel to transform yourself into someone you're not. The uniqueness of your human operating system is powerful, especially once you truly understand how it works.

In all the Digs I've done, I've met a handful of people who share the same Dig word, but I've never run across two people who have the exact same HOS. Each of us is unique, and each of our operating systems is a fingerprint of our own soul, a blueprint of our own essence.

There are patterns, of course. Certain words tend to gravitate toward each other, like "justice" and "courage" or "curious" and "grow." There are also patterns in the way operating systems emerge visually, which we'll get to in a minute.

But no matter the collection of words or shape of expression, each operating system is unique to the person who embodies it. Each of us experiences the frequency of various words in a different way, because we all bring a lifetime of experience, perspective, and meaning to our HOS. The way we live it, express it, and apply it to our work, relationships, and decision-making is utterly singular.

And that's what makes this work so powerful. Too often, we fall into the trap of comparison, believing that if someone else has a similar purpose, vision, or drive, then ours must be less special or less valuable. But that couldn't be further from the truth. There is no redundancy in human existence. We are not here to fit into predetermined slots. We are here to express something only we can express. There will never be another person who has your story and your HOS! Our world needs each of us to show up fully in our own way.

Finding our uniqueness isn't just about being special for the sake of it. It's about getting clarity about your role in the world and embracing it with confidence. It's about efficiency, too. When you align with your operating system, decisions become easier, struggles make more sense, and you stop wasting energy fighting against who you are.

And just as importantly, you stop beating yourself up for not being someone else. Too often, we think we need to be more logical, more structured, more bold, more reserved—whatever it is we assume we're lacking. But when you see your operating system reflected at you in its purest form, you realize you don't need to be anything other than who you already are. The real work is in aligning with it and owning it.

OWNING WHAT MAKES YOU TICK

Steph Davis's operating system doesn't just take her to the edge—it inspires her to leap off it.

She's a professional free climber, BASE jumper, and wingsuiter, known for scaling some of the highest peaks imaginable and soaring off them. It's obviously pretty dangerous—or at least that's my perception. Steph's perception came through loud and clear when I coached her for her TEDx Talk.

Her operating system is built around autonomy, risk, nature, and a fierce rejection of the things that make most of us feel safe: stability, predictability, and approval. (And railings at the edges of tall cliffs!)

But even though Steph's operating system doesn't always mesh with the world around her, she's been a pioneer both in extreme sport and building a career around it. She's earned sponsorships and become well-known as an athlete, but she's also lost so much along the way.

We worked together on her TEDx Talk, "Choosing to Fly," not long after her husband, Mario, died in a BASE jump in Italy. He crashed into a point on the mountain mid-flight and didn't survive. Steph had jumped first and landed, expecting him to be close behind. She didn't know what had happened to him until a helicopter recovered his body. It forced her to reevaluate everything in her life, including life itself.

In her speech, she told her story with clarity and courage, and she challenged her audience to reconsider their own relationship with risk.

"What's funny to me is how we always talk about taking risks like it's an option, or a decision we get to make," she said. "Like there might be some version of life where just getting out of bed doesn't open you up to an endless gamut of risks." She went on to explain that there's no way to avoid risk in life, ending with "The real risk is in making your life small and turning your world gray."

Is danger found in doing what you love, even when it involves risk? Or is it in living a life that's safe but never fully yours?

For Steph, the right path will always be doing what she loves—not because it's easy, but because it's the only way she knows how to be. Her operating system won't let her settle for anything less, and every time she climbs to the edge and leaps, she's living in the full truth of who she is.

As Steph writes on her website, "The fear is the danger."

If your soul is your essence, your HOS is how you express that essence. Which means that understanding your operating system is like finding the key that unlocks your soul. That's the magic of this process. It's a reminder that we are all rare, irreplaceable unions of traits, experiences, and instincts. And the more we honor that, the more we can bring our full power into the world.

The challenge with unique operating systems is that everyone else has one, too—and they don't always mesh. Two people can share the same experience but walk away with completely different perspectives. What one person finds inspiring another might find overwhelming. What feels like a simple request to one person might feel like a major imposition to someone else. It explains why conflicts arise, even when no one is trying to be difficult.

Unless your operating system has driven you to be a hermit living on a remote mountain, you'll frequently find yourself in situations where you have to compromise: with other people, with your work or family, with the larger culture in which you live. Life isn't always neatly aligned with your HOS. Relationships, jobs, responsibilities—they all require negotiation. Sometimes the things that once fit you perfectly start to feel like they don't fit at all. So what do you do when you can't change your external circumstances?

This is where alignment becomes an *internal* practice.

My client Pam understands this better than most. She's a long-distance athlete whose Dig word is "Equilibrium," and her operating system is all about balance. For Pam, that doesn't mean everything in life is always balanced—it means she knows how to *find* balance, no matter what's happening. Over the years, she's faced devastating losses: a cancer diagnosis, the death of a husband, struggles with her family. She didn't have the power to force those destabilizing events back into balance—no one does. So, rather than trying to control the uncontrollable, Pam focused on what she *could* influence: herself. She leaned into the practices that kept her steady. She kept running, literally putting one foot in front of the other. She stayed present. She remembered her purpose, and she found ways to live in equilibrium and balance, no matter what life threw her way.

As the old adage says, "If you want to change the world, change yourself first." That doesn't mean faking positivity or forcing silver linings. It means choosing alignment *within* yourself, even when the outside world refuses to budge. And it all starts with remembering who you are and what makes you tick.

REMEMBERING YOUR HOS

There's a reason I've been using the word "remember" when talking about your operating system. This process isn't about creating something out of the blue, or picking answers on a personality quiz. It's about *remembering* what has always been there. Remembering is powerful. It strips away the noise, the expectations, and the pressure to be something you're not. When you remember your operating system, you stop searching for clarity in everything around you and realize it's been within you the whole time.

As we'll discuss in chapter 6, your Dig word isn't something you choose, like a new value or a fresh identity. It's not something you manufacture or aspire to be. It's simply been with you all along, quietly shaping your choices, your reactions, your deepest desires and frustrations. When people finally land on it, it often feels more like recognition than discovery.

In chapter 4, you examined the stories of your life to find patterns and themes, distilling key moments down into powerful truth words that capture the core of how you operate. At this point, you should have a cloud of descriptive words on sticky notes. But they're no longer just sticky notes. They're soul catchers. Mirrors that reflect the truest parts of yourself.

In this step of the Dig, we're going to take those words and distill them even further until we arrive at the purest form of your truth, homing in on the words that are most potent and useful to you. Take this opportunity to revisit the words you've chosen—and even push back on them a bit. Are the words you've chosen really describing what's at the heart of your human operating system? Get as specific as possible, and keep scratching to get beneath the surface.

We might label someone who has navigated several scary events as "inspiring," but *why* are they inspiring? Maybe it's the "courage" they displayed during those hardships, or the "persistence" they consistently brought or the "creative" way they transcended their circumstances.

"Freedom" is another common word that I view as an opportunity to go deeper. I often find you can get a lot more specific and interesting if you keep asking yourself: Freedom to do what? In my case, it's freedom to be authentic. In Nick's case, it's freedom to have fun. In Erica's case, it's the freedom to do what feels good.

And some people, like Steph, need freedom for freedom's sake.

We're aiming to distill your HOS down to about ten words, which I've found is the sweet spot at this stage. That gives you enough to play with as we find the shape of your OS, but it's not too overwhelming. If you have fewer than ten right now, great. But if you have more, I recommend trying to distill them down a bit.

For some people, this step can be extremely difficult. They want to get it correct the first time, and so they get caught up in making sure they've chosen the "right" words. But this isn't about being right or wrong. It's about feeling into the patterns, the cycles, and the energies that move through your life. Think of this process as what bestselling author Anne Lamott famously calls the "shitty first draft." It's about allowing the first version to be far from perfect but totally real.

This process is messy, uncomfortable, and absolutely necessary—so be bold enough to claim a first draft of your operating system.

1. Look for Overlap and Synonyms

Do you have multiple words that express nearly the same idea? For example, if you have both "adventure" and "explore," ask yourself if they serve different functions in your life or if one naturally includes the other. If one word feels broader and encompasses the other, keep the more expansive word—remove the other sticky note from the table, whiteboard, window, or other surface you're using to build your HOS.

One of the biggest traps people fall into is getting stuck on the word itself. Words carry baggage. They can be branded into our minds. Sometimes a person will reject a word outright because of past associations. The key is not to let the word distract from the truth it's pointing to. We're using words because they help us shape something abstract into something we can own, work with, and share.

As you sift through, remember that it's about the *frequency*, not the word itself. Don't get hung up on the literal meaning of a word, or any connotation (whether positive or negative). In fact, if you're having a strong reaction to the word, that might be a good sign that it holds power in your operating system.

A client of mine who had struggled with being overweight found words like "big" to be rather triggering. After all, her size was the thing she battled her entire life! But once we were able to see "big" as a frequency that also encapsulated her business, marriage, and other ease-filled aspects of life, she was able to really embrace it.

Tune in to your Resonance Meter and ask why that word is speaking to you or repelling you. When you hit on the right frequency, it will resonate with you and you'll know that word belongs in your HOS (at least for now).

2. Group Words in Categories

Many words can be clustered under broader themes. For instance, "create," "innovate," and "imagine" might all belong to a larger theme of expression. "Matter," "meaning," and "impact" also fall under their own group theme.

Begin to sift through the sticky notes in front of you, grouping them by instinct into categories. Then spend some time with each category to see if some words are more resonant than others. You might find that "create," "innovate," and "imagine" each speak to a subtly different part of your operating system. Or you might decide that they're close enough together to eliminate one or more.

If that's the case, tune in to your Resonance Meter to determine which best represents your essence. Consolidating a set of words or keeping them separate will just feel *right* when you get it right.

3. Look for Words That Feel Like You

Your operating system should be a representation of how you show up in the world. Ask yourself: Do I actively embody this word in my daily life? A well-rounded operating system reflects all aspects of who you are. Do your words include elements of both personal and professional life? Do they reflect both how you think and how you act?

Go through your list and ask: Which of these words sparks the most recognition? The goal is to identify words that feel undeniably *you*. If a word makes you sit up straighter or gives you a sense of excitement or relief when you see it, it's likely a keeper.

4. Test by Elimination

Some words will feel absolutely essential, but you might not understand that until you take the sticky note off the table. One effective technique is to temporarily remove words from your list and see how it feels. Does eliminating a word make you feel unmoored? If so, bring it back. If a word disappears without much reaction, it may not be as critical as you thought.

If removing a word would leave you feeling misrepresented or incomplete, that's a strong sign it belongs in your operating system.

5. Make It Up

There are times when no matter how hard you try, there simply isn't a word to communicate the frequency you're trying to capture. In those situations, invent one! Because it's more about the frequency than the word itself, you can absolutely take liberties with the words as you see fit. It's *your* life purpose, after all!

One of my clients, Keri, was struggling to land on a word that captured the duality of nature. Nothing we came up with had a frequency that encompassed both the raw edge and radiant splendor of *aliveness*. So we made up a new word: "Tenderwild." It lit up Keri's face as soon as she heard it, and I knew we'd found a winner. Years later, Keri embraced her love of nature by getting her very own Sprinter van with a TNDRWLD license plate!

Another client, Bobby Stuckey, is the co-owner of a Michelin-starred and James Beard Foundation award-winning restaurant in Boulder called Frasca Food and Wine. What sets Bobby apart from other restaurateurs is a deep devotion to his guests' experience of Frasca's venue and fare. He thinks of every guest who comes through his door as family and embraces them (often quite literally) as such. Hospitality is everything to him—but it's a very specific kind of hospitality. It is quintessentially Italian. During his Dig, Bobby came up with the word "Hospitalian" as his one-word purpose. Later, we crafted a TEDx speech called "Be a Hospitalian" to help others learn this skill.

6. Write "I Believe" Statements

List your potential HOS words and write an "I believe" statement for each. For example, if one of your words is "connect," you might write, "I believe we are not meant to live this life alone, and the relationships we cultivate define who we become." If one of your words is "rise," you might write, "I believe we each have the ability to rise above our surroundings and shine our brightest lights out into the world."

Don't overthink this, and don't edit—just let it flow. In fact, it can be helpful to set a timer for ten or fifteen minutes and use the time pressure to tap into your instinct. After all, your first response is often more truthful than something you've spent a lot of time wordsmithing.

When you're done, read your statements aloud and pay attention to how each one feels. Do you feel a physical response? A sense of clarity or shift in energy? When I'm Digging a client, I listen just as much to the way a client's energy spikes or drops while they're reading as to the words themselves. That can be a powerful clue to which words are resonating with them. You can do the same for yourself. Record yourself reading your "I believe" statements, or ask a trusted friend to listen as you read and to reflect what they hear.

7. Keep Refining Until It Feels Right

As you explore your operating system, you might even find yourself adding new words or playing with synonyms. That's all okay! For example, maybe one of your words was "comfort" but as you work, the word "ground" or "home" comes to mind. You can write the new word on a new sticky note, or even jot it down as an alternate on the "comfort" sticky note until one of those words emerges as a clear winner on your Resonance Meter.

Your words should feel like a clear, confident statement of who you are. Once you have your set, sit with it for a few days. If something still feels off, tweak until it fully resonates.

By the end of this process, you'll have a powerful, distilled version of your truth—one that can guide your decisions, actions, and growth with clarity and intention.

THE METAPHOR OF SHAPE

As you sort through your words, you might start to see a shape taking form in the way you've organized them:

- a pyramid with a grounding base and far-reaching peak
- a staircase that stretches upward, with specific steps
- a human body shape with words representing the legs, trunk, and head
- a cycle that has a linear order and is circular in shape
- a series of columns that look like a strand of DNA
- a math equation that balances neatly or adds up to something

If a shape has started to present itself, pay attention to it. A shape metaphor is a powerful way to bring your operating system to life by transforming a collection of truth words into something tangible and making it easier to understand. Think of a metaphor as a symbolic representation of how you move through the world.

Some operating systems take the shape of natural elements, like a tree that grows tall when rooted in fertile soil. Others might be directional, such as a rocket launching into the sky, symbolizing momentum and breakthroughs.

I've mentioned before that I've never seen two people with the same human operating system—even if they share a Dig word. But I have seen similar shapes emerge. I know this can all seem a bit abstract, so let me give you some examples to help guide you. Of course, this isn't to say that you need to aim for something like this! Instead, it's to share with you what's possible, so you can come up with your own.

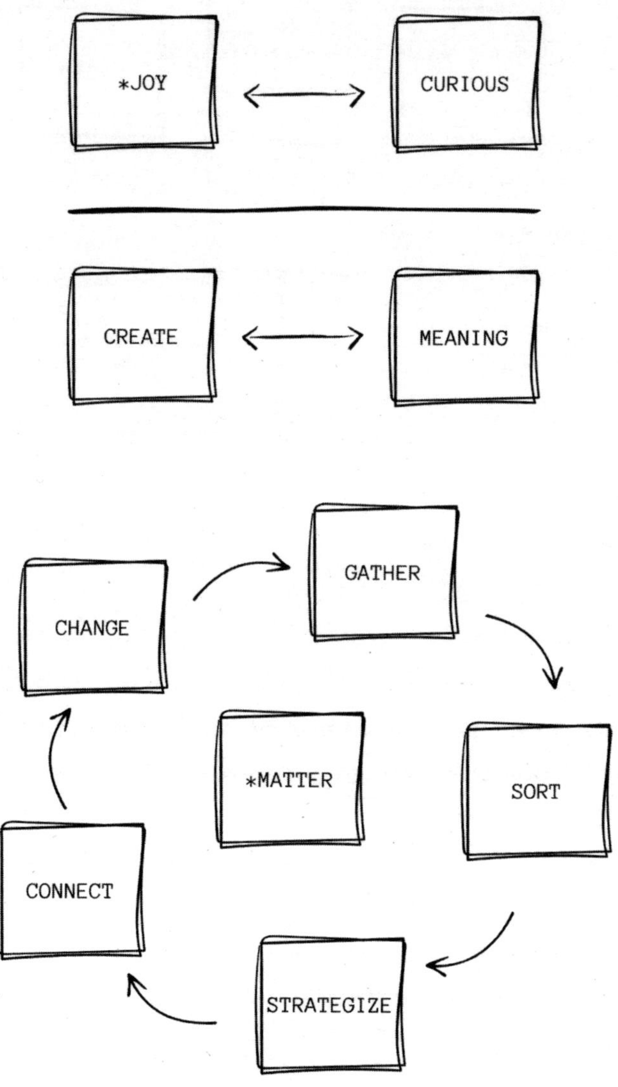

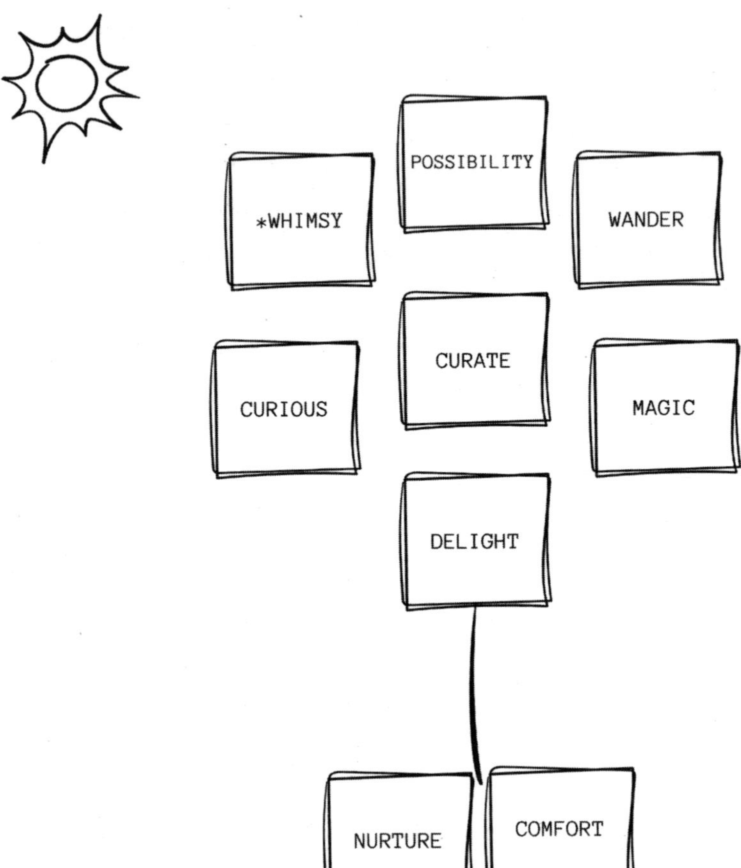

If your previous work didn't already reveal some kind of shape, explore now to see if one presents itself. The key to finding your metaphor is tuning in to the energy and movement of your truth words. Ask yourself:

- Does my system feel like it flows in a continuous cycle or moves in a straight direction?
- Is there a natural or structural shape that embodies my core values?

- What imagery instinctively comes to mind when I think about how I operate?

For example, if your truth words emphasize resilience, adaptability, and transformation, your metaphor might be a river—steadily flowing forward, navigating obstacles, and reshaping the landscape over time. If your words reflect stability, grounding, and support, your metaphor might be a mountain—solid, enduring, and unshakable.

Other shapes you might explore:

- Cycles: circle, spiral, clock face
- Structures: tower, ladder, path, pyramid, columns
- Mathematical: network, equation, spectrum
- Nature: flower, tree, animal, human, river
- Abstract: explosion, geometric shape

There's no wrong answer here! Your words may support each other like building blocks. They may flow into each other as part of your process. They may ground you; they may help you soar. For example, I've always thought of mine as a hawk, with a central core and a pair of wings spreading out to either side.

The important thing is to play until you feel that little voice in your soul say, "Oh, hey. I recognize that."

Spend some time exploring your operating system, until it starts to feel familiar. It can help to step away and come back the next day—but don't get hung up on this step. Remember, we're not going for perfection here, and *you* are the one who decides what's right! The draft of your operating system will continue to change as we work through the next chapter.

TAKEAWAYS

- Your human operating system is the internal framework that guides how you interact with the world—like a computer's OS, it runs everything in the background. It's made up of your core values and habitual ways of functioning, and no two people have the same HOS.

- Living in alignment with your HOS brings ease, joy, and fulfillment. Even small misalignments can create subtle discontent. Big misalignments in jobs or relationships can deeply affect your well-being. Once you know your HOS, it becomes a guide for better choices that lead to a more aligned life.

- Your operating system is consistent over time, but it's not a box. You can still grow and adapt while honoring it. For example, if your HOS values "freedom," you might still thrive in a structured job—as long as there's space for authenticity and autonomy. Your HOS points to how you function best, not what path you must take.

- Steps to Clarify Your Operating System

    a. **Look for Overlap and Synonyms:** Eliminate redundancy by keeping the broadest or most resonant word.

    b. **Group Words in Categories:** Notice which words naturally cluster and refine based on resonance.

    c. **Identify Words That Feel Like You:** Focus on what sparks energy or recognition.

    d. **Test by Elimination:** Remove words and notice which feel essential.

    e. **Make It Up:** When there is no word to accurately describe your vibe, invent one!

    f. **Write "I Believe" Statements:** Articulate your beliefs around each word to test for emotional truth.

    g. **Keep Refining Until It Feels Right:** Tweak as needed until the list reflects your core identity.

- As you finalize your OS, you may begin to see a visual shape or metaphor (like a tree, a staircase, a river, or a hawk) that reflects the energy and structure of your truth. This helps you conceptualize your operating system as something alive and actionable—a symbol of how you move through the world.

CHAPTER 6

UNCOVER YOUR WORD

By this point, you've distilled a lifetime's worth of stories into truths: single words that represent your nonnegotiable phrases, core values, and resonant frequencies. You've condensed those words into the ten or fewer you suspect of working together as your operating system, and you've organized them in a way that is starting to feel familiar to your very soul.

Now it's time to uncover your Dig word.

Think of the operating system like a sports team. You can't play the game without all the players—but there is one captain, and that's your Dig word. The one word that rules all the others. The word that's calling the shots.

If your operating system is the "how" behind the way you move through the world, your Dig word is the "why." It's the true motivator, the unseen force pulling the strings behind the choices you make, the passions you pursue, and the frustrations that make your blood boil.

I've worked with thousands of people to uncover their Dig word, and the moment they recognize it is always powerful.

When we hit on someone's Dig word, everything shifts.

Sometimes the tears start, or the deep exhales begin. Maybe they just loosen up, the tension in their face and shoulders finally relaxing as their energy settles down. Their spine might straighten or their eyes go wide. The energy in the room becomes electric. It's impossible to know how this reaction will show up with each person, but it does—every time.

This is one of the most powerful ways I know to recognize your Dig word: It hits you on a visceral level. The body knows. That physical or emotional experience is the confirmation that truth has been uncovered, sometimes even before the brain catches up.

What's really fun is when someone has the self-awareness to recognize that shift in themselves, and I get to watch them work out in real time what's going on. Maybe they've been trying to make another word fit. Maybe they've been dancing around their most powerful match because it's uncomfortable. But when they recognize that energetic shift, there's no choice left but to lean into it.

When you're going through the Dig process on your own, you need to be more self-aware than if you're working with a partner who can reflect those changes to you. Before you go through this chapter, take a moment to really tune in to your body. Do a meditation, go for a walk, or revisit the Resonance Meter (chapter 2) to calibrate how you're reacting.

Then, as you work, pay extra attention to your physical and emotional reactions to each word—especially if you have a negative reaction. The word that annoys you, that feels too vulnerable or reminds you of someone you can't stand? That's probably the one you need to pay attention to.

Sometimes your Dig word is the one you secretly hope it's not. I've had so many clients push back when we start to circle a particular word, and I'll just gently invite them to stay with it a little longer. Because usually, that resistance is data. It means the word is stirring something up—and that something is worth exploring.

So, if you're doing this work on your own, pay attention to how your body reacts as you explore your potential Dig words. Are you leaning in or pulling away? Do you feel a surge of fiery energy—or a lump in your throat? These feelings are guideposts. And your truth is usually waiting right behind them.

In my case, when I landed on the word "authentic," it lit up like a neon sign through every memory of my life. The battles I'd picked throughout my youth were always about being authentic. The work I did around safety with Girls Fight Back was about helping women live authentically. The TEDx Talks I helped people prepare were about tapping into their authentic messages.

Once I saw it, I couldn't unsee it. It explained why I never cared about just saying something—I had to say it with full honesty and integrity or not at all. It explained why I feel physically uncomfortable when I have to sugarcoat my words or hedge my opinions. If I can't be fully authentic, I'd rather stay silent.

And believe me, authenticity has gotten me into trouble more times than I can count. It's strained relationships and been a source of friction in past jobs. There have been so many times in my life that I wished I could have filed that part of my personality down in order to make things easier on myself. But the complexity of my relationship with the word "authentic" is exactly what makes it the perfect Dig word. I could feel it in my bones, that complicated mix of understanding and resignation.

That was—and is—my biggest struggle in a nutshell.

I've seen this moment of clarity strike again and again in my clients. Some people instantly embrace their word. Others resist it. Some even hate it. But without fail, every single person I've worked with has eventually come to see their Dig word as an undeniable truth—a thread woven through every decision, every challenge, and every success in their lives.

I've worked with clients whose Dig words changed the entire course of their careers. Some realized they were in the wrong job, the wrong relationship, or the wrong city. Others saw that they were already doing exactly what they were meant to be doing; only after Digging did they fully understand why.

When you find your word, you gain clarity. You see why you've been drawn to certain paths and repelled by others. And, just as importantly, your Dig word gives you insight into your struggles. It shows you why you've felt stuck, why you've made the same mistakes over and over, why certain fears or frustrations have held you back. Your Dig word isn't just about what makes you great—it's about what makes you human in all your messy, complex, honest glory.

THE COMPASS AND THE CHALLENGE

Your Dig word is never just your strength—it's also your Achilles' heel. It's what you're best at, but it's also the thing that trips you up, over and over. It's the thing you most crave—and the thing that, when it's missing, hurts the most. It serves as a guide or a compass. It is also your lifelong challenge.

For Jennifer Brown, a diversity, equity, and inclusion strategist, that word was "Power." When we hit on it, she flat-out said, "Oh no. I do not like that word. This is everything I fight against."

My response was "Exactly."

Jennifer had spent her career fighting against traditional power structures, challenging authority, and advocating for the marginalized. Power, to her, was something oppressive, something to dismantle. And yet, the more we talked, the more she saw how power had shaped everything in her life—not just externally but internally, as well.

Jennifer, you see, is a Trojan horse. She identifies as a queer cisgender woman, and thus a member of the kind of marginalized communities she advocates for. She's also white, blond, and conservatively dressed in her public appearances. She blends right in with traditional corporate environments (while she doesn't choose to, she can "pass" in these environments) and knows how to speak their language. After her Dig, she realized her work is actually about slowly, stealthily manipulating and shifting power distribution.

As she told me, "I realized how central power really is to my work—my own power, the power of women, and the power of people who remain underrepresented in the corporate spaces I move through. It's not just about resisting power anymore, it's about redefining it."

For speaker and entrepreneur Jasmine, the word was "Enough." She's a striver. A business badass who has so much to share and give. From the outside, she looks like she has everything dialed in—but internally she's been on a lifelong mission to realize that everything she does and everything she *is*, is enough. She's been chasing that word her entire life.

When she walked into my office for her Dig, I remember noticing how tired she was. She was used to pushing through fatigue, to persevering, to succeeding. But she was exhausted by the version of success she'd achieved, which wasn't authentic to her operating system. No matter how much she'd done, she still felt like she was falling short, that she had to do more, prove more, be more. The moment she saw her Dig word, she knew. It wasn't just something she needed—it was something she was here to *embody*. Something she could help others understand in their own lives.

Another client, Adam, is the front desk manager at a tech repair shop. His word is "Worth," and he carries it into all his interactions and decisions. He sees worth in every customer who walks through the door with a shattered cell phone screen, and is driven to make sure they get the high-quality service they deserve. He's not interested in putting in effort if the worth of the activity or relationship isn't immediately evident.

For this reason, he comes across as a pretty intense guy. While attending one of my workshops, Adam was able to recognize that the anger issues that plagued him his whole life were consistently triggered by feelings of unworthiness and insecurity. This knowledge presented him with a choice: keep flying off the handle and alienating people, or consciously make the effort to stop the self-hatred spiral and finally start seeing his inherent value. In shifting his perspective, he was able to create a different reality for himself and others.

That's the dual nature of a Dig word. It's both your compass and your challenge. It's the thing you stand for but also the thing you struggle with. Your superpower and your shadow. Understanding the duality of your Dig word gives you the opportunity to choose how you want to show up in the world.

I know. That's a big ask for a single word.

But here's the thing: When you name your Dig word, you own it. Instead of being at the mercy of this invisible force that's been steering your life since childhood, you can start to work with it. You hopefully become the master of it! You can recognize the patterns, the triggers, the way your word shows up again and again.

You might even feel seen.

BEING SEEN

For many people, uncovering their Dig word can feel like someone shining a spotlight onto their very soul. As you can imagine (or maybe you're even starting to discover, if you're getting close to recognizing your own word), this experience brings with it profound relief—and profound discomfort.

In Dr. Sona Dimidjian's case, her Dig Word felt like it clashed with an important part of her identity: her career as a psychological scientist.

When Dr. Dimidjian and I started working together, she was preparing to give a speech with His Holiness the Dalai Lama. Yes, *that* Dalai Lama. So, as with all of my clients, we started with the Dig. At the end, we landed on a single word: "Love."

Dr. Dimidjian wasn't convinced. "Sorry," I told her, "but that's your word." (I don't remember being quite that direct, but Dr. Dimidjian does. She's probably right.) I just knew it.

It took Dr. Dimidjian a while to agree with me. But in the end, she saw that love was the consistent thread that was woven throughout her story and her life's work.

Now, over ten years later, she's the director of the Renée Crown Wellness Institute, which conducts research to promote the wellness of young people—and infuses love into everything they do. By emphasizing "respect, humility, kindness, and dignity" in their approach, the Crown Institute blends science and love, two things that historically haven't been talked about together.

Matt, a motivational speaker, had felt invisible for most of his life despite building a successful career being in front of an audience. Matt was born without legs, which meant he not only had to navigate a world that hadn't been built for him but also had to endure the way most people looked away rather than looking at him. Multiple times during his Dig, he mentioned the quick glances, the averted eyes, the awkward attempts to pretend he wasn't there. He said that when people did look at him, it wasn't always in a way that felt human. Sometimes he saw pity in their eyes. Sometimes curiosity. But rarely, if ever, did he feel true recognition.

When we did his Dig, we uncovered the word that had been at the core of his entire experience: "Seen."

At first, the word hit him hard. He had spent a lifetime not being seen, even while he was up onstage, sharing his story and advocating for accessibility and inclusion. On the surface, he was already visible. But there's a difference between being seen and being *seen*. By uncovering his Dig word, Matt understood that every speech he gave and every conversation he had was an opportunity to help people understand what it meant to truly see one another. To look beyond surface differences, beyond discomfort, beyond assumptions, and help others feel as seen as he wanted to be.

While Matt was relieved to recognize his word, others don't always find it so comfortable. Katie, a pediatrician and lifelong seeker of truth, danced around her word during her Dig for a long time before finally letting it land. Her word was "Heal." In many ways, she had been living it her entire life—but accepting it required her to see herself more clearly than she ever had before. Katie's story of healing began long before she ever set foot in a medical school classroom.

She was born in Vietnam in the middle of war, her earliest years shaped by trauma, upheaval, and survival. Her parents carried deep wounds from their own pasts, the kind that quietly echoed through generations. Even as a little girl, Katie was deeply attuned to her own pain and that of others. She didn't just want to help people feel better; she felt compelled to restore what had been broken.

At one point, we explored lighter, more uplifting words for her operating system—options that felt shinier and easier to claim. But no matter where we wandered, we kept returning to "Heal." Eventually, Katie softened, breathed, and nodded with a quiet certainty. "Yeah," she said. "That's it."

Accepting "Heal" allowed her to recognize what her life had been pointing to all along: She wasn't put on this earth merely to treat illness or mend symptoms. She is a healer of people—physically, emotionally, and spiritually.

Our Dig words carry a duality. Healing had defined Katie's life, but it was also a wake-up call for herself. For Katie, recognizing her Dig word wasn't just about understanding her purpose—it was about finally allowing herself the space to heal, too.

A DOUBLE-EDGED SWORD

Austin Eubanks was just seventeen when he found himself hiding under a table in the Columbine High School library. His best friend was hiding next to him, and when the gunfire stopped, Austin was alive—but his friend was gone. The same bullets that took his best friend had struck him, too, hitting his hand and knee, but the physical wounds were nothing compared to the emotional devastation that followed.

In the aftermath of Columbine, Austin was prescribed painkillers for his injuries. But while his physical pain was at a three or four, his emotional pain was an absolute ten. And, as he said in his TEDx Talk, "Opioids are profoundly more effective at relieving the symptoms of emotional pain than they are at relieving the symptoms of physical pain."

Austin fell into an addiction spiral for the next decade, until he finally faced the trauma he'd been running from and found his way to recovery. And when he did, he committed himself to helping others do the same. By the time I met Austin, he had become an advocate for addiction recovery, working in treatment centers, educating people about trauma, and helping others heal from the kind of pain he knew all too well. He was invited to give a TEDx Talk about his experience, which is when we started working together.

As part of the process, we did a Dig. I expected his word to be "Heal," given his work and his message. But it turned out to be "Help."

As Austin explained it to me, there was a profound difference. Healing is internal, personal. Help is what we offer one another. Help is showing up. It's standing by someone's side, even when you can't fix the problem. It's being a loving presence, without attachment to the outcome.

Austin's lesson came at an important time for me, because at the time, my brother Brian was deep in his own battle with addiction. I had experienced years of pain while watching him struggle, wanting so desperately to fix things for him. But Austin had made something clear to me: *Healing my brother wasn't my job. Helping was.*

Understanding that distinction gave Austin clarity about his role. He couldn't take away people's pain. He couldn't erase trauma. But he could help, and so could I.

For that last year of Brian's life, I stopped trying to change him or heal him. Instead, I met him where he was. We had real conversations, unfiltered by my expectations of what he should be doing. I focused on the moments we had instead of worrying about the ones we might not.

And when Brian died of cirrhosis at the young age of forty-five, I didn't have to wonder if I had done enough. Because I knew—I had helped the best way I could, by loving him without conditions. By seeing him exactly as he was. By being present, even when it hurt.

But "help," like any Dig word, was Austin's double-edged sword. Austin had built a life around helping others, but when he needed help himself, he didn't know how to ask for it. He had embodied the role of the person people turned to, which made it harder than ever for him to admit he was also struggling.

Six weeks after speaking on a panel at a live event I was hosting, Austin died of an overdose. No one saw it coming. He had been doing the work, living his purpose, making a difference—and yet, in his darkest moments, he couldn't reach out for help the way he had encouraged so many others to do.

His death absolutely wrecked me. It made me angry that he couldn't ask for the very thing he had dedicated his life to giving. Angry at how addiction steals people too soon. Angry that someone with so much wisdom, compassion, and strength still struggled under the weight of his own word.

But Austin's legacy lives on. His TEDx Talk, titled "What Surviving the Columbine Shooting Taught Me About Pain," continues to be watched by thousands, helping people long after he's gone.

I know this is a heavy story. In fact, I know a lot of the stories I've shared in this chapter are heavy. Many are both uncomfortable and existential. But I want to be absolutely real about how important this work is—for yourself and for the world around you. Once you uncover your Dig word and recognize the role it's played in your life, you won't be able to unsee it. But you *will* be able to embark on a life-long journey to do the work that word requires of you.

The world is waiting for you to embrace your superpower. More importantly, *you* are waiting. Are you ready?

UNCOVERING YOUR DIG WORD

The process of uncovering your Dig word is different for everyone. Some people land on it like a lightning strike; some come to it more gradually. One—or several—of the following exercises might help you get closer. Remember, you'll know you've got it when you feel a sense of recognition (which might also be coupled with relief, frustration, and/or resignation).

1. Find the Cornerstone

Go back to your operating system and play around some more with the shape. Consider more deeply how the words play with each other within that shape, and try to identify which word belongs in the foundational spot of that shape, like the center of a circle, the keystone of an arch, the grounding point of a column, the pinnacle of a pyramid.

Try different words in this position, exploring the ways they subtly change the meaning of your operating system. Does one feel more true than the others?

2. Journaling

In the last chapter, you wrote "I believe" statements—brief descriptions of each word in your operating system, focusing on how it resonates with you. Now revisit those statements and find places to explore deeper through journaling. Keep a sharp eye out for words that are challenging for you, since that can often be a sign that they are an extremely powerful part of your operating system.

You might also begin to explore the relationships between words in your journaling. How do they lead to each other, enable each other, support each other? Where are the harmonies and the contradictions?

Another good journaling exercise is to return to the stories of your life, which you outlined in chapter 4, with your human operating system in hand, and journal about the ways it has influenced you in key moments. Focus on asking what facets of your HOS were at play and why.

3. Triggers and Superpowers

Look at each word in your operating system and ask two questions: Does this word trigger me? and Does this word feel like a superpower? The Dig word will usually resonate with both of those questions.

It can help to turn your attention outward here and think about the things you admire—or get frustrated by—in others, because these are often a reflection of how you feel about your own traits. Where do you notice overlap in the positive and negative aspects of those traits? For example, maybe you admire your friend's organizational prowess while also routinely being frustrated by her perfectionism. Or maybe your colleague's complete lack of awareness of deadlines drives you crazy, even while you grudgingly appreciate their ability to effortlessly pivot into creative solutions.

Finish these sentences: "I admire people who..." and "I absolutely hate it when people..." What patterns emerge? How do they resonate with the words in your own operating system?

4. Through-Line Check

Remember, your Dig word isn't just a recent value—it will be a through line in your life, present as a driving force for as long as you can remember. Keeping your operating system in mind, what themes and patterns do you see recurring through the stories? Look at your list and ask:

- Which of these words comes up the most when I reflect on my life story?
- Which word is at play in every major life event—my successes, failures, moments of clarity?
- If I had to remove all but one word, which one feels non-negotiable?

5. Try It on for Size

Pick a word from your operating system and try it on for size. Say out loud: "My Dig word is ______." Notice your body's response. Do you feel tension? Resistance? Recognition? Where on the Resonance Meter does this word hit for you? Which word makes you feel energized? Emotional? Which word, when spoken, feels like coming home?

You might even take a week and spend each day sitting with a different word. Write it on a sticky note and keep it with you, checking in regularly to see how you feel about it in different situations.

TYING YOUR OPERATING SYSTEM TOGETHER

If you've gone through these first three steps—telling your story, remembering your human operating system, and uncovering your Dig word—you've given yourself an incredible gift. Most people feel a strong sense of recognition once they've gotten here. It's like the different parts of themselves—their stories, their purpose, their struggles, their superpowers—have finally clicked into place in a way that makes sense.

It can be a real epiphany moment for many. Maybe it has been for you.

And if you stopped the Dig process here, and you closed the book and stepped back into real life, that sense of calm or being seen would probably be quickly swept away by the demands of your jobs, families, friends, and other obligations. Maybe you've had that happen in the past, after doing other self-help work. I certainly have!

That's because knowing how your operating system works isn't useful if you don't choose to operate from it on a daily basis. Identifying your Dig word is just a neat bit of trivia if you don't put it into practice again and again. We can only be fully authentic to ourselves if we choose to be there in the first place—but that's a huge challenge when faced with real life.

It's a good thing the Dig process isn't over yet!

Telling your story, remembering your operating system, and uncovering your Dig word are just the first three steps of the Dig process. The final step will take all the incredible work you've just done and tie it together in a way that will continue to make a lasting, positive impact on your life and help you share your message with those around you.

TAKEAWAYS

- You've distilled your story into ten or fewer powerful words—your human operating system (HOS). Now it's time to identify the single word that encapsulates your core purpose. If the HOS is the how, the Dig word is the why. It acts as the captain of your team of truth words, the underlying force driving your life.

- The Dig word brings clarity—but sometimes a little discomfort, too. Many people initially resist it because it holds both their greatest strength and their most vulnerable challenge. It's what they crave most and what hurts the most when it's missing. It is your superpower and your Achilles' heel.

- Uncovering your Dig word can feel like being truly *seen* for the first time. It brings deep validation but may also resurface emotional difficulties. Some embrace it immediately; others struggle. This is only natural. Your word mirrors a lifelong journey, and that journey will have had its highs and lows.

- There's no one right way to uncover your Dig word, but you'll know it's right when it feels like both relief and challenge. Trust your body and intuition to signal when you've found the word.

CHAPTER 7

WRITE YOUR MANIFESTO

The Dig is about increasing your self-awareness and giving you tools to make decisions. It'll help you navigate situations in ways that are true to your human operating system so you can spend more time in the flow of life and less time mired down and unsure about what to do next. But it's *also* about propelling you to effective action, day in and day out. That's why the final step is to write out a manifesto that incorporates everything you've learned about how your operating system works and what you want to accomplish.

You've done the hard work to unearth your truth. Now it's time to put it into a form that will keep you focused, inspired, and aligned. Think of your manifesto as a piece of armor or a shield. It's a talisman. A warm and cozy blanket. It's your North Star that guides you ever forward—or whatever imagery speaks best to your operating system. It's the thing that will help you remember what you learned from your Dig so that when you inevitably return to the real world and come face-to-face with the usual challenges, you'll have something to remind you of your Core truth.

Whether you write it, paint it, or turn it into a piece of art, your manifesto is meant to be visible, tangible, and deeply personal. When life inevitably gets messy, it will be there to help you stay the course.

The Latin word "manifestum" means "clear, apparent, or made visible." You probably won't be surprised to learn it's the root of the word "manifesto"—as well as "manifest," a word that can get bandied about a lot in self-help books. These two words work together perfectly in this case.

A manifesto is a clear and public declaration of an individual's or group's beliefs or intentions, and for centuries, manifestos have been used to declare revolutions and spark social change. From political revolutions to avant-garde art movements, manifestos serve as bold claims about what truly matters. A good manifesto makes things "clear, apparent, and visible." It pulls Core truth out of the shadows and holds it up for all to see. *This is who I am. This is what I believe. This is what I stand for.*

The first manifestos were political—like *The Communist Manifesto*, written by Karl Marx and Friedrich Engels in 1848. In the early 1900s, artists began using manifestos as a way to define cultural movements and challenge the status quo. The Futurist Manifesto, the Dada Manifesto, and the Surrealist Manifesto were all written within a couple of decades of each other, taking the political format and creating emotional, imaginative, rule-breaking declarations in the name of art.

Social movements also embraced manifestos as tools of liberation and resistance. Feminists, Black civil rights groups, workers' rights groups, LGBTQ+ groups, and others have issued manifestos to voice their frustrations and paint their version of a more equitable future.

Manifestos are so powerful because they're not just a statement of belief—they invite action. They lay out an argument and ask the reader to become a collaborator in a possible future. You might even say they ask the reader to help *manifest* their version of that possible future.

As a verb, the word "manifest" means "to make something real or visible." In self-help books, you'll hear people talk about manifesting your vision by using mindfulness, intention, and focused thought to align your inner world with the outer one to bring your vision into reality. This is work we've been doing all along in this book (and we'll dive even deeper into that in chapter 8).

If a *manifesto* is a statement of truth, *manifesting* is the act of turning that truth into lived experience. In both cases, you're using words, imagery, and intention to bring the unseen into the seen and breathe life into it.

How powerful is that?

Today, manifestos have become personal. Individuals use them to inspire themselves. Companies use them to declare their purpose and values. You've probably seen one on a brand's website, a coffee shop's wall, or an influencer's Instagram page. These aren't calls for revolution in the traditional sense—but they are still calls to live with clarity and conviction.

My colleague Anita Stubenrauch is responsible for the Apple Credo, a 171-word statement that begins, "We are here to enrich lives. To help dreamers become doers, to help passion expand human potential, to do the best work of our lives." (While "credo" and "manifesto" are often used interchangeably, a credo is generally a statement of belief whereas a manifesto is a statement of action.)

Anita was asked to take the project on in 2014, when, as she writes in a Medium post, it had become clear that the original credo didn't encapsulate the growing business—and that it had been revised over the years until it was a tactical document rather than something that inspired.[1]

Over the next year, Anita was part of a team at Apple who used surveys and focus groups to help them understand what was at the heart of the company. They uncovered something surprising,

Anita writes. People weren't looking for the credo to say a specific thing or use specific words. They needed it to make them feel a certain way.

Even as society has changed rapidly in the past decade, the Apple Credo has stood the test of time. Why? Because Anita future-proofed it. The credo sets the sights out of reach, reminds readers of their best selves, and speaks galvanizing truths. Tactics may change over time. Strategies may shift. But strong vision has staying power.

As she writes, "Whether your vision is expressed in a few words or a few thousand, if it's written to stand the test of time, it can be a tool to powerfully aid your aspirations, however audacious they might be."

In this chapter, we're going to tap into the power of manifestum to turn your Dig word and human operating system from abstract concepts into calls to action. You might emblazon this manifesto proudly on your website or office wall for all to see and be inspired by—or this statement might be for you and you alone. However you choose to use this manifesto in your own life is up to you. The important thing is that you don't skip this step.

Let's get real here for a minute. How many self-help books have you read where you had an epiphany that felt life-changing in the moment but that you can't remember now? How often have you picked up a new book, or signed up for a new course, hoping that this one will *finally* turn everything around for you? How much money and time have you spent on self-improvement, only to still feel like that next big epiphany is just around the corner?

I've certainly been there, so no judgment!

I'm not trying to imply that this book is the be-all and end-all of self-help books. But I think what a lot of them are missing—and, to be honest, what a lot of us *miss doing* when we read through these books—is a final step of integration. The step where you take the work you've just completed and internalize it in a concrete way.

That's what we're doing here.

This final step of the Dig is your opportunity to get specific. To get bold. To name what's true and claim it for your own. It's your opportunity to ensure all the work you just did isn't going to wash away like a sand castle in the tide as soon as you close the book. Because, let's face it. This work is never done.

In the Disney movie *Moana*, Moana is a wayfinder—a practitioner of the ancient Polynesian practice of using the stars, the planets, and the waves to navigate the open ocean. She's not turning on her GPS and kicking back; she's always recalibrating her path based on the sky.

Your human operating system and Dig word are those starry skies above. They will guide you, but they don't work like a GPS. You have to continually check your path and compare it to the truth you've remembered in this work. And your manifesto is how you'll find your way. Ready? Let's get started.

STEP 1: WRITE A DIG STATEMENT

If you're like most of my Dig clients, you probably felt a moment of deep recognition when your human operating system started to come together. Hopefully you felt seen, or like the various puzzle pieces that make up your life had clicked together with a satisfying *snap*. It felt good, right?

Now, imagine you've told your grandma or your nine-year-old nephew that you've been reading this book and doing this work. Or maybe you recommended the book to a coworker or a barista—someone who doesn't know you well and isn't ready for a deep dive into all the epiphanies and revelations you might have had over the last few chapters. When you say you've learned all about your operating system, they'll probably ask, "So…what did you figure out?"

What will you tell them?

Or maybe you're coming back to this work after some time away, and now you're staring at the stack of sticky notes that make up your HOS. You remember the profound sense of relief you felt when you originally worked this all out, but now these sticky notes are only vaguely familiar. *They formed a circle, right? Or was it a tree? And what did that signify to me?*

Whether explaining what makes you tick to a friend or remembering it for yourself in the future, you need a simple, clear explanation you can easily remember and share. I call this a Dig statement. Basically, a Dig statement is a quick-and-dirty explanation of your operating system that uses simple, clear language that anyone could understand.

Don't worry about writing a beautiful essay here! You're not going to enter this in any writing contests. Just jot down the first phrases, words, and language that come to mind—those are often the most raw and closest to the truth. All we're doing here is telling a brief story about how your operating system works, in a way that's useful to you, so that when you return to this work next week, next month, or even years from now, you have a clear, concise explanation of your HOS.

Let's take a look at some examples:

Life should be all about having fun, living adventurously and doing epic shit. Gathering, sorting, connecting, and strategizing for change are the path to what matters—and what matters is the JOURNEY.

Shine your light! Live with whimsy. See the possibilities. Wander constantly. Get curious about the magic that's all around you. Find your delight. And know it's okay to seek comfort and be nurtured as well as care for others.

It all starts with choice. Choose possibility! When you do, you'll find that more good is possible, more exploration is possible, more curiosity is possible, and then more momentum is inevitable! This is what gives you freedom and allows you to share your truth with others.

Each of these examples incorporates the words of their person's human operating system and encapsulates the general flow of the operating system's shape. None of them are going to win a Nobel Prize for literature. They don't always use proper grammar, or even complete sentences. That's okay! You can always polish things up later, but right now, write out your Dig statement. It should take five minutes, tops.

STEP 2: GATHER YOUR "I BELIEVE" STATEMENTS

Once you have a rough Dig statement, the next thing you're going to do is go back to the "I believe" statements you wrote in chapter 5. Originally, the purpose was to help you explore the words you were considering for your operating system and see how they all fit together. Now we're going to mine them for phrases, insights, and sentiments we can use in your manifesto.

Because you wrote the "I believe" statements before finalizing your operating system, some of them may be about words that didn't make the cut. Give those a quick glance to see if there's any language or phrases you'd still like to include in your manifesto, then set them aside.

Next, take the statements that did make it into your operating system. Arrange them in an order that makes sense and is as true as possible to your operating system. (Hint: Your Dig statement will be a good guide here!)

As you read through the statements, start highlighting phrases you love and anything that hits high on your Resonance Meter. This is all excellent fodder for your manifesto! You might also note any areas that you would like to explore more deeply. This is a good opportunity to get more clarity by journaling, talking it out with a friend, going for a walk to record a voice memo, or however else you like to collect your thoughts.

This step might only take a few minutes if you feel like you're pretty clear on your operating system and "I believe" statements. But feel free to slow down here and take time to explore more deeply if that's what feels right to you.

If you did any other journaling while working through the earlier steps of the Dig, you can mine that for phrases and ideas, too.

STEP 3: DRAFT YOUR MANIFESTO

Now it's time to bring it all together to create a single powerful statement.

I know we've used a lot of lofty language in this chapter about speaking your truth and inspiring action in others—so you may be feeling a lot of pressure to make this manifesto completely encapsulate you. But it doesn't have to be perfect right off the bat. In fact, do you remember the "shitty first draft" mindset we talked about earlier? This is an excellent time to adopt that mentality.

You might feel like you've nailed it immediately, or you might spend the rest of your life returning to the draft, tinkering with it to make it spot on. Either way is totally fine. The important thing is getting started.

Though I *will* say that there's such a thing as tinkering too much and editing out the rawness and personality that makes your manifesto so true and powerful. Have you ever read a corporate manifesto, for example, and felt like it was pretty blah? As someone who's worked with a lot of companies on manifestos, let me tell you that they normally start out pretty powerful—they just sometimes get edited down by committee until all that's left are milquetoast platitudes that won't offend anyone.

The best manifestos, in my opinion, are the ones where the raw passion and emotion are still just below the surface. After all, even if you do decide to share your manifesto with the world, it's for *you first*. Don't worry too much about pleasing your high school English teacher or making it socially acceptable! This is the time to fully own your truth.

Here are my rules for writing a strong manifesto:

1. Keep it short. I tell my clients to aim for 150 words or less—we want your manifesto to be concise, clear, and punchy. This is deceptively hard. At this stage, you've probably recorded or written thousands of words, from telling your story to writing your "I believe" statements to journaling. Now I'm asking you to distill everything important into a handful of sentences. Just remember, this is all about cutting away the fluff and getting to your absolute truth. You don't need any long explanations here, just punch lines.

2. Write from the Core. This manifesto is your truth, unapologetically claimed. Use active, powerful language and keep your sentences short and direct. No hedging or softening your statements with words like "maybe" or "I think." No dialing down your message with passive phrasing—and definitely no apologies! If it helps, go back through the Head-Heart-Core exercise in chapter 3. The passion and straightforward desire of the Core is what we're looking for here.

3. Stay simple. The magic of a manifesto comes from honesty and clarity, so don't complicate things! Pay attention to places where you're using filler words, repeating yourself, overexplaining, or justifying yourself. Watch out for places you're using fancy multisyllable words when simple ones will do.

4. Use strong verbs. Your manifesto is not a wish list—it's a statement of who you already are. Pay attention to your verbs and look for places where they could be stronger. For example, instead of "I try to…" say "I commit to…"; instead of "I want to…" say "I will…" or "I do…" Use active, energetic language that gets to the point. As Mark Twain famously said, "The difference between the almost right word and the right word is the difference between the lightning bug and the lightning."

5. Be yourself. Finally, your manifesto should sound like you. If you're someone who speaks with passion and intensity, let that show. If you have a calm, steady energy, reflect that in your writing. If you like flowery language, go for it! If you need to pepper it liberally with four-letter words, you do you. In your manifesto, of all places, you should feel free to be yourself.

EXAMPLE MANIFESTOS

To get you started, here are some examples from my clients. Note that while they have different tones, each is clear, direct, and deeply personal. They're full of vivid words, short and punchy sentences, and—most of all—incredible passion.

Chris, a West Point grad and former public servant:

I want each of us to win.

I embrace what I care about and release everything else.

I am fanatically driven by IMPACT.

My motto is: See, Serve, Solve.

I allow my light to shine.

I own my freedom and never abandon my faith.

Today I strive to be better than yesterday.

Tomorrow I'll be better than today.

Climb higher. See farther. Let's go!

Jesse Lee Gray, a writer and creative:

I am here to manifest magic. To lean into the unexpected—in the momentary mundane and the wild blue yonder. To receive what's revealed with wonder.

To be the fire that burns away the inessential. To put purpose into words and bring big ideas into action. To find a way around whatever blocks the path.

To you, my fellow travelers I say

Open your heart and lead with it. Own your shit (mud and lotus)! Build your community with care—one relationship at a time.

Get curious, connect the dots, and invest wholly in what you choose. Let everything else go.

Be brave. Step up and step forward with whatever you've got today.

Go out on a limb and stay there. Walk with the wobble. Embrace the bounce. If you fall, get up. If you fail, learn and keep going, confident in your purpose.

Step into the light and dare to be seen, moving ever closer to the world you want to see.

Let's do this—ONWARD!!

Joe, a communications executive:

Seek to understand. There is no better gift than to be seen and understood. Every person you cross has something to teach you, and every moment offers something profound and transformative. Lean into the awe-inspiring truth that all things are delicately interconnected. Focus on what you can control and let the rest go. Your intuition is your hidden superpower. Live in harmonious flow, expressing your internal and external self. This is your truth. Stay curious. Be drawn in by depth, and bring calm to the chaos. Humble yourself. Heal in nature. You are human. Trust your heart as a hopeful romantic. Embrace your individuality. You are built for connection, love, truth, and encouragement. You're a listener and a storyteller. Drop in. Stay open. Face the wave. On to the next mistake. You are perpetual perspective. Together is better. You are a self-aware social chameleon, and that is your vibe. Time is all we have and it, too, shall pass. Make your words matter while you're here. Move people with your message. Show your authentic self in every relationship. Don't be wasteful with time, energy, opportunities, or people. Don't take life too seriously. Grace lives in the gray. Thrive as a child of variety. Create music. Find your flow. Your ripples will make waves.

STEP 4: BRING YOUR MANIFESTO TO LIFE

Now that you have a draft of your manifesto, how does it feel? If it's this powerful as a collection of sentences written in your journal or stored on your hard drive, imagine how much more powerful it could be as a work of art.

Even if you're not a particularly "artistic" person (and I would argue that we're all artistic in some way), you can still bring your manifesto to life. Create a poster using a graphic template, or make a collage with magazines and newspapers. Compose your own personal theme song or create an inspiring video montage. The point is to craft something that pleases you aesthetically and place it somewhere you will see it every day, like in your bedroom, on your bathroom mirror, or above your desk. You want it easily visible so it can inspire you and remind you that this is how you want to show up in the world and what you hope to accomplish in this one short, beautiful life.

For me, it started with sticky notes.

When I work with clients in person, I write down their words, phrases, and themes on sticky notes during the Dig (just like you probably did). Each of those little sticky notes contains a tiny piece of my client's soul, so at the end of every Dig it seems crass to throw them away. Instead, I started tucking each stack of notes into a plastic sandwich bag with the Dig word on top, so that I could see at a glance whom it belonged to. (I have a freakish memory for the Dig words of everyone I've ever worked with.)

Eventually, I pinned many of those sandwich bags into a grid on my office wall as a reminder of the incredible people I've worked with. It's kind of like hanging out with a bunch of my friends, and it's a cool visual about how our lives fit together in a beautiful—if chaotic—whole.

But at some point, I was inspired to do more with these thousands and *thousands* of sticky notes I've collected over the years. So I started creating art pieces based on people's Dig words.

One of my first projects was for my friend Rosalind Wiseman, whom I talked about in chapter 4. Her Dig word is "Worth," and I wanted to create something that visually captured the depth of that concept. She's an author, and her book *Queen Bees and Wannabes* definitely deals with the topics of worth and worthiness, so I started by layering pages from her own book as the foundation. Over that, I collaged images of money from all over the world, symbolizing the way worth and value—both personal and financial—are so closely tied. I painted the whole thing in a wash of pink and orange and yellow because Rosalind is such a colorful person, and the final piece was bold, vibrant, and deeply personal. Just like her.

Another piece was inspired not by a single Dig word but by the frequency of the community my clients represented. I used the Dig words from sixty-seven people, handwritten by each of them on sticky notes, to spell the word "WE" on a giant canvas. The idea is that when a viewer sees it from across the art gallery, that's the only word they can make out. But as they get closer, the large "WE" dissolves into dozens of individual words representing all the unique and amazing individuals who can come together collectively to make anything possible!

Words are powerful. But when you combine them with art to create something unique to you, your manifesto transforms from words into a constant, unshakable reminder of who you are and what you stand for.

Here are some ideas to help inspire you. If you'd like to see visual examples head to erinweed.com/justoneword.

1. Create a Handwritten Poster

There's something powerful about artistic handwritten manifestos—I have a whole Pinterest board devoted to them! It doesn't matter how beautiful or chaotic your handwriting is, I think it always looks amazing when turned into a manifesto poster. Plus, the act of writing things out by hand helps cement them in the brain in a way that typing them out can't imitate.

Grab a large sheet of paper or poster board and any pens or markers that call to you, and channel your inner child. You can write your manifesto linearly from top to bottom. You can spiral it inward—or outward. You can jot each phrase haphazardly in a vivid jumble, if that's what feels right to you.

Decorate your poster with stickers, glitter, paint, magazine cutouts, and anything else that calls to you.

2. Create a Hand-Lettered Wall Hanging

If you want to get a step fancier and you enjoy lettering or calligraphy, consider writing your manifesto in a decorative script and turning it into a framed piece or canvas painting. Use brush lettering, ink, or even embroidery to write out phrases from your manifesto (or the whole thing). To make it even more artistic, experiment with gold foil, metallic pens, or bold colors to make certain words pop.

Here's a tip for those of us who aren't professional calligraphers: Even if you're not skilled at hand-lettering, you can print out words in a font you like and either trace them or use stencils to achieve a nice hand-lettered effect.

3. Design a Digital Print

Is the idea of a handwritten manifesto giving you flashbacks to elementary school art projects—and not in a good way?

If you prefer a clean, professional design, consider using a graphic design tool like Canva or Photoshop to turn your manifesto into a beautifully designed digital print (or hire a professional designer). This lets you choose the fonts and colors that reflect your personality, add imagery and design elements that inspire you, and create a unique piece you'll love.

Then you can print it all out at your local print shop on high-quality paper that gives your manifesto a polished look.

Sallie, a consultant in the carbon management space, had her manifesto professionally designed:

DR. SALLIE GREENBERG

```
Manifest your life. Matter, because you do. How does this
resonate? Have fun. Live adventurously. Do epic shit.
Change the conversation. Use your superpowers for good,
not evil. One life, one meeting. Let go of the past, live in
the present, trust in the future. Connect with what matters.
Feed your soul. Align with your truth. Breathe. Do things that
scare you. Be a spark. Show up. Have plans. Embrace the
journey. Your role is clear: Speak truth and be strategic. Seek
clarity. Run in the rain. Memorize the feeling. Live with
no excuses, travel with no regrets. Adventure is always a good
idea. Seek fulfillment - don't chase happy. Let go of what does
not serve you. Refuse to dull your shine. Say yes! Ask yourself
often, "What kind of old lady do you want to be?" Be a badass.
Embody your operating system. Head, heart, core. Hold the pen.
Unlock the genius in the room. Love your own company. Use your
wings. Be a maker. What you do matters.
```

4. Make a Collage or Vision Board

Who says your manifesto needs to contain words at all? If you're a more visual person, try creating a collage-style manifesto by grabbing a stack of magazines and cutting out images and colors that reflect the feeling and energy of your statement.

You can turn it into a multimedia piece by grabbing one of those shadow-box frames from a craft store and adding fabric swatches, pressed flowers, stickers, and found objects that help give your manifesto art depth and meaning.

5. Paint a Mural or Chalkboard Wall

For those who like big, bold statements, why not paint your manifesto directly onto your wall? Paint your Dig word and key phrases as a giant mural, decorating it with artistic elements, symbols, and patterns that resonate with you.

Or try turning one of your office walls into a giant chalkboard using chalkboard paint, then adding your Dig word in giant letters as a focal point and writing your manifesto around it.

6. Record an Audio or Video Version

Not all art has to be physical! If you're an audiophile, consider recording a voice memo of yourself reading your manifesto or creating a short video of you speaking your truth, set to music or meaningful visuals. You could also write a song or create a meditation track you can turn to when you need a moment of alignment.

Listening to your own voice declaring your manifesto can be an incredible reminder of your power.

7. Design a Tattoo or Wearable Art

Do you want a daily reminder? Why not turn your manifesto into something wearable! Engrave a piece of jewelry with a meaningful word or image. Design a T-shirt, tote bag, or coffee mug that you can wear or use regularly as a reminder of your purpose. There are a ton of print-on-demand sites where you can upload your design and have a one-off item made relatively inexpensively.

Or you could go even more permanent. Several of my clients have gotten tattoos of a key phrase or symbol from their manifestos. Joe, whom I mentioned earlier in this chapter, got a tattoo of his word, "Perspective"; another client, Susan, tattooed her word, "Awake." Another chose a pair of ornate sewing snips as a reminder of how making hard choices and cutting away unneeded threads is what enables her to embrace her word, "Possibility."

8. Let Your Imagination Go Wild!

The possibilities are endless! If you're always on your phone (and who among us isn't guilty), try designing a lock screen or background that incorporates your manifesto. Or set up alerts to pop up daily to remind you of important lines.

You could schedule yourself a series of postcards to be sent quarterly, or leave yourself sticky notes throughout the house. Plant your garden so when the flowers bloom each spring they form your Dig word, or hire someone who owns a plane to write it in the sky every morning! (Okay, that last one might be a bit much.)

The point is to create a version of your manifesto that you love looking at or experiencing on a daily basis. It should feel like a true representation of you—whether it's sleek and modern, messy and expressive, or bold and unapologetic. A piece of art that inspires you to live your truth.

However you choose to bring your manifesto to life, make it yours in a way that becomes a living, breathing part of your daily life. Your manifesto isn't meant to be tucked away in a journal, forgotten after a moment of inspiration. It's meant to be something you return to again and again to guide your choices, align your actions, and remind you of who you are.

TAKEAWAYS

- The final step of the Dig is turning your discoveries into a living, actionable reminder. Your manifesto acts as a talisman, shield, or North Star—keeping you aligned when life gets messy. It turns personal truths into calls for action—clear, public declarations that manifest your internal work into reality.

  - **Step 1: Write a Dig Statement.** Create a simple, accessible description of your human operating system, focusing on language that's easy to understand and emotionally resonant. Imagine you're explaining what you just learned to your grandma or to a nine-year-old.

  - **Step 2: Gather Your "I Believe" Statements.** Review your earlier "I believe" exercises from chapter 5, highlighting resonant phrases and insights that can fuel your final manifesto.

  - **Step 3: Draft Your Manifesto.** Distill everything into a clear, short statement (150 words or less). Be concise, write from the Core, use strong verbs, be simple, and sound like yourself.

  - **Step 4: Bring Your Manifesto to Life.** Turn your written manifesto into a tangible daily visual reminder: a handwritten poster or hand-lettered wall art, a digital print, a collage or vision board, a mural or chalkboard wall, an audio/video recording, a piece of wearable art, or even a tattoo! Your imagination is the limit.

PART III

ALIGN YOUR LIFE

CHAPTER 8

NAVIGATING VIOLATIONS: THE HEART OF CONFLICT

I was the first person to build a house in my neighborhood. At the time, there was nothing here—just open land and promise. It felt a little like living in *Little House on the Prairie* but with indoor plumbing, which was both cool and kind of terrifying. But there was a huge draw: I got to design my home from scratch.

As someone who values authenticity, being able to express myself through my home is incredibly important to me. One of the reasons I chose this particular development was because of how much variety they offered in the types of home they built—it wasn't going to be a cookie-cutter community. I was excited to customize my house, and I had a blast choosing the architectural details and paint colors that really spoke to me and setting up a cozy front patio where my kids and I could hang out and enjoy Colorado's spectacular sunsets.

Eventually, more people started moving in. The neighborhood began to grow. And after about two years, a man built a house across the street from me...in the *exact* same style as mine.

Okay, sure. There are only so many architectural styles and layouts, so this was bound to happen. But he'd also chosen all the same design details. I was grumpy, but I told myself it was fine. Maybe my customization wasn't as unique as I'd thought it was. I'm a grown-up. I could get over it.

Then the owner painted his new house the *exact same colors as mine.*

Now I was annoyed. As the first neighbor here, I'd been a huge supporter of the development, going so far as to open my home for tours. In fact, this person had toured my home and commented how much he loved it. Apparently, enough to steal every detail! Couldn't he think for himself?

I told myself I was overreacting—until the day I looked out my window to discover my new neighbor had bought the exact same patio furniture as mine. There was no denying it; he was copying my house.

To some, this might seem petty. It's just a house, right? Just furniture. But with an operating system like mine, this person's lack of originality felt deeply offensive. It wasn't just that he'd copied my home—it felt like he'd stolen my expression of self. I'd made deliberate choices to create something unique, and now I couldn't look out my window without feeling like that had been taken away.

My frustration went deeper, though. I've made it my life's mission to help people express their authentic selves, and copycats and plagiarizers aren't expressing themselves with integrity and grace. They're not tapping into what's true for them; they're expressing what's true for someone else and diminishing the originality of the person they've stolen from in the process.

Now, someone with a different operating system might look across the street and shrug. But for someone with mine, tromping on my creativity and the uniqueness of my home—especially so geographically close to it—was a violation.

What do I mean by violation? Well, pull up a chair, friend. Because I *love* talking about violations.

THE JOY OF VIOLATIONS

Someone makes a rude comment in the coffee shop. Your partner forgets to grab something you asked for from the grocery store—again. Your employer announces a new policy that seems objectively ridiculous. How many times has something rubbed you the wrong way and you told yourself that you were overreacting, you were too sensitive, and you should just get over it? How many times has someone *else* told you that?

Because these triggers are so personal, it's easy to feel like we're being irrational when we react to them. But when you consider that the things that trigger us the most are actually violations of our operating systems—our core selves—the intensity of the reaction begins to make sense. Violations aren't just irritating. They actually attack something fundamental about who we are.

It's almost like violations are flashing Vegas-level neon signs that show what's most important to us.

Violations can show up in different ways—in our relationships, our jobs, and our environments. They can be small, temporary blips in our harmony, or they can be long-running, deep-seated issues. When we experience a negative reaction toward something, it doesn't mean that person or situation is inherently bad. It just means it's going against who we are at our core. And recognizing that gives us the power to do something about it.

Let's say your operating system values beauty and serenity. Sitting in a crowded, ugly airport with a nearby baby crying so loudly that it cuts through your noise-canceling headphones is a violation—albeit a temporary one. Landing back home in the chaotic, overcrowded, noisy city you relocated to for work, though, is a violation that will grind at you day after day.

Or maybe your operating system values integrity and fairness. If you overhear one of your coworkers tell their spouse a white lie over the phone, the violation will eat at your sense of right and wrong. And if you're working in a place where you're encouraged to cut corners day in and day out, you'll probably start to feel like everything you believe in is being eroded.

In either situation, you're not being overly sensitive or uptight. The things that piss us off the most and evoke the biggest reactions do so because they go against who we are and what matters most to us. That's no small thing.

But these moments of friction can *also* be some of our greatest teachers. They force us to see our own values more clearly. They help us refine what truly matters to us. And sometimes, they challenge us to grow in ways we never expected. At least, that's what we experience when we take a deep breath, slow down, and approach the violation with curiosity.

Recently, I was asked to present about authenticity at a conference. I was initially excited about the opportunity—from the outside, it seemed like an organization and community that would be super aligned with the work I do. But once I was actually at the conference, I felt enormously disconnected from the people around me. In conversation after conversation, I got the sense that most people there just cared about looking good in the world rather than being truly authentic. By now, you probably understand just how triggering that can be for me.

At first, I was frustrated. I felt constricted, unable to fully express myself in an authentic way because I didn't feel safe being so vulnerable in this group. But rather than getting angry or irritated, I decided to shift my perspective. Instead of seeing the people at this conference as obstacles or railing that they were going through life in the wrong way, I chose to see them as teachers.

I had a choice: I could sit in judgment, irritated that they couldn't just *be more like me*, or I could approach them with curiosity. What was driving their desire to present a "perfect" version of themselves to the world? What could I learn from them? And maybe—just maybe—what could they learn from me?

At the end of that trip, I left with a deeper understanding not just of the people I met but of myself as well. I saw my own values more clearly. I recognized where I could be more flexible, more compassionate. And I also reaffirmed the importance of surrounding myself with people who shared my desire to live their most authentic lives.

Being in violation with others doesn't have to mean conflict. It can mean clarity. It can be an invitation to look deeper at ourselves, at others, and at the lessons waiting to be learned.

WORKING WITH VIOLATIONS

Violations are at the heart of conflicts between loved ones, colleagues, and companies. Yet frequently, instead of targeting the root of our conflict, we try to solve satellite issues. It's no wonder we can't make progress! One of the greatest gifts of the Dig is that it makes it easier to spot the violation right away and expend your efforts solving that problem, not an ancillary one. It lets you name what's going on so you can claim it.

There are always going to be violations in life. Even if you manage to create the most serene, untriggering existence possible, you won't be able to avoid them. But you *can* learn to navigate violations more easily and craft a life that doesn't go completely against the grain of your operating system.

In the next two chapters, we'll craft personalized tools designed to help you quickly access your human operating system in moments of stress in order to bring yourself back into alignment. But first we need to understand what we're up against. We need to get good at recognizing a violation and taking steps to keep it from becoming a trigger, which becomes an emotion, which becomes a downward spiral that devours your entire day (or week).

When you develop the ability to stop, examine the violation with objectivity, and make a different choice to reset your course, you'll have an incredible superpower.

Step 1: What Exactly Is the Violation?

It's shockingly easy to spiral into a bad mood when something triggers us. And unless we're paying close attention at the time, it might not be easy to spot the moment when things went off the rails.

A conversation over dinner with a friend might leave you feeling irritable instead of connected. A text from your boss might launch you into a mental roller-coaster ride of anxiety. The state of your kitchen when you walk in to make your first cup of coffee might set your dial to a frequency of overwhelm before you've even had a chance to fully wake up.

When you notice a stormy feeling, stop and name it. Be specific. Instead of just saying, "This person is driving me crazy" or "This job makes me miserable" or "I hate my apartment," pinpoint what exactly feels wrong. Is it your friend's refusal to try a new restaurant that's driving you crazy? Is it the constant last-minute meetings that are making you miserable in your job? Is it the sad beige paint on your kitchen walls that makes you hate your apartment?

Identify *exactly* where your good mood jumped off the rails, and name it.

Step 2: Why Is This a Violation of My Operating System?

Once you've figured out what exactly is bothering you, turn your attention to why this situation feels like such an attack. What is it about your friend's refusal to eat somewhere new, the last-minute meetings, or the sad beige paint that grates against your operating system?

Maybe your operating system values exploration and novelty, which is why spending time with someone who won't budge from their comfort zone is so aggravating. Even though you love your friend, their lack of adventure makes you feel claustrophobic whenever you hang out.

Maybe your operating system values deep work and focus, and the fact that your coworkers are constantly adding last-minute meetings to your schedule disrupts your flow and destroys your ability to concentrate on the work at hand.

Maybe your operating system values vibrancy and energy, and the sad beige walls are making your apartment feel as soulless and bland as a corporate office. No wonder you feel so uninspired and overwhelmed whenever you're at home.

Be specific, and keep asking "why" until you hit on the core reason this thing bothers you so much. (The 5 Whys exercise in chapter 4 is a good one to use here.)

Step 3: How Is This My Responsibility?

Recently, I met a friend for lunch. She stormed in, apologizing preemptively for her bad mood. It turned out someone had flipped her off in traffic, which she knew was a small moment in the grand scheme of her day, but she was struggling to let it go. As we talked, she realized the reason the rude gesture bothered her so much was because it had jolted her out of her flow—and her operating system is all about being in the flow.

She wasn't necessarily upset with the other driver. She was frustrated at being thrown off-kilter. But we kept asking questions. Did the violation *start* with that other driver flipping her the bird? Clearly, if she'd done something in traffic that warranted that response from somebody, she was probably already out of the flow. If she were to take radical self-responsibility, she'd recognize that she was already distracted by her busy morning and should have taken the time to center herself before she even got behind the wheel.

Taking that kind of radical self-responsibility is hard to do. It's much easier to think that the outside world is always at fault—but when we do that, we give the outside world a huge amount of power over us.

Don't ever give someone the power to ruin your day. Be the hero of your own movie.

Step 4: How Can I Reset My Course?

Now that you've identified the specifics of the violation and taken some radical self-responsibility for it, the final step is deciding what to do about it and how you'll move forward.

Let's go back to our example of the person with an operating system based on beauty and aesthetics who's elbowing their way through a busy airport to return to their chaotic home city. In both cases, the violation is an external situation that can't be changed. Airports are gonna airport. Chaotic cities are just going to stay noisy and busy.

Maybe this person will eventually choose to take a different job that lets them work remotely from wherever they like best, or they'll move to a quieter neighborhood that vibes better with their operating system. But for now, they can choose to create an oasis that gives them a retreat from the noise and lets them maintain their serenity.

And they can also choose to get curious about the ways the external situation *does* match their operating system. After all, there are moments of beauty and serenity in every chaotic situation. This hypothetical person has the choice to let those moments get overshadowed by the greater chaos or to seek them out and find them even more wondrous because of the environment they exist in.

When you're in a violation, ask:

- **Can the external situation be changed?** You might set healthier boundaries, leave a job, move to a different environment, or have a hard conversation, for example.
- **If not, what internal shifts can you make?** Try reframing your mindset, clarifying your values to better understand the violation, or shifting your focus to where you're in alignment with your HOS.

Sometimes, no matter how deeply a situation violates our operating system, we simply *can't* change it. Maybe we're in a job we need to keep for financial reasons. Maybe we live in a place that isn't ideal but is necessary because of family obligations. Maybe the violation comes from a person we love and want to keep in our life.

Or, like my friend who got flipped off, maybe the *moment* of violation is now in the past. We can't go back and change what happened, but we're still stuck stewing over it in the present.

When external change isn't possible, the question becomes: *"How can I exist in this violation while staying true to myself?"*

Step 5: What Can I Learn?

We can't always change the situation, but we *can* up-level our understanding of how we see and navigate the world. We can learn to have compassion for people who do things differently than us. In some situations, we can also embrace our role as a teacher. We might not be able to sway someone to our point of view, but we can be more mindful about how we embody a healthy frequency and be a good example to others.

We're all students of the world and the people around us. If we can be constantly curious and approach violations in the spirit of learning and teaching—instead of a spirit of combativeness—we'll all come out better for it.

Going back to my neighbor's house, I knew I had a choice. I could stew in my frustration indefinitely, or I could delve deeper to understand why this situation had such a grip on me.

That's when I had an unexpected epiphany.

Yes, I was angry at his lack of originality. (Still am, if I'm being honest!) But the situation also forced me to ask whether this house was actually my most authentic expression. I realized I had an entire Pinterest board filled with dark, monochromatic homes—sleek black exteriors and dramatic wood accents. I absolutely love that aesthetic, but I'd never given myself permission to make such a bold choice. Maybe my house wasn't actually the fullest expression of me.

Suddenly, my neighbor's house didn't bother me as much. Instead of feeling like my expression had been stolen, the violation showed me where I had been holding back. It was a reminder that I had room to go deeper into my own authenticity.

MAKING BIG MOVES

Sometimes, a violation isn't just an everyday frustration—it's a sign that something big needs to change. We've talked before about how unsustainable it is to live out of alignment with our operating systems for the long term. But sometimes it can take a rock-bottom moment—a job loss, a divorce, a financial crisis, or an emotional burnout—to get us to see how badly we need to make a change.

No one wants to hit rock bottom. But there's more than suffering at the bottom—there's also clarity. It's about losing the ability to go back to the way things were, so we're finally forced to move forward instead.

Well before I met Brandi, she founded a beauty company while living in a domestic violence shelter. She was only twenty-one years old, but she already had a strongly developed operating system built around the word "Protect"—and she'd spent years living in an abusive relationship that was a direct violation of that core value.

Finally, after a particularly dangerous incident, she found herself in the shelter. Everything had fallen apart. She had lost her sense of safety, her sense of stability—everything except the one thing she had ignored for so long: her need to *protect* and to *be protected*. That moment of crisis led her to build a company centered around empowering and protecting others. She channeled her experience into something that not only helped her heal but gave purpose to her life. Today, her business funds domestic violence shelters and provides support to women in need.

Another client, Scott Strode, hit rock bottom on his bathroom floor during a drug- and alcohol-fueled binge one night. His heart racing, he became convinced he was going to die. And he couldn't stop thinking that someone was going to have to tell his mother that her son had died on his bathroom floor. The next day, Scott decided to get sober.

His Dig word is "Choice," and his addiction was robbing him of his ability to choose a better possibility for himself and his future. While in recovery, Scott realized how important it is for those struggling with substance abuse to dream about what's possible—it's what helps them keep choosing sobriety again and again. He founded a sober active community called The Phoenix that connects people who want a sober lifestyle, giving them a way to stay aligned and on track.

You don't have to hit rock bottom to realize it's time for a change. But you *do* have to pay attention to recurring violations that aren't going away. Are you constantly drained by your work? Do you feel out of place in your current environment? Do you repeatedly face conflicts in a relationship that seem impossible to resolve? If the answer to any of those is yes, it might be time for a big shift: a career change, a move, a reevaluation of the people in your life.

When we refuse to acknowledge our violations, they rarely resolve on their own. They manifest in other ways—stress, burnout, resentment, emotional exhaustion. They seep into our relationships, our work, our mental and physical health. Over time, they can lead us so far out of alignment that we don't even recognize ourselves anymore.

The good news is that understanding exactly what is in violation of your operating system can provide you with a custom road map to finding a path out of it—hopefully without hitting rock bottom first.

STEADY ON THE PATH

In the next chapter, we'll start building your own personalized tools to help bring you back into alignment with your operating system. The more you do this work, the more you'll find that addressing violations, whether big or small, brings an enormous sense of relief. It's an incredibly powerful feeling—but it can come as a shock to those around you.

Not everyone will cheer you on when you decide to shift your priorities, set new boundaries, or step into your full potential. The biggest source of resistance might even come from those who are closest to you: partners, friends, family members, or colleagues who have gotten used to who you've been and aren't sure who you're becoming.

One of the hardest things I've ever had to do was step away from a friendship. Society tells us that certain relationships are nonnegotiable. That no matter what, you work it out, you stay connected, you keep showing up. But what happens when someone close to you is in direct and constant violation of your operating system?

For years, I tried to make it work with a close friend of mine. I wanted to believe that we could find common ground, that things could change. But every interaction felt like a battle between who I truly was and who I had to be around her. Every time I spoke honestly about my life, my work, or my passions, it seemed to trigger something in her. I could feel the shift—her discomfort, the subtle digs, the way she'd twist my words or undercut my accomplishments. At first, I made myself smaller and walked on eggshells around her. But the more I did this, the more I realized I was betraying myself just to maintain the relationship.

I tried every possible way to make it work—conversations, compromises, you name it. She didn't want to do the work, and at some point, I had to accept that. I finally stopped trying to fix what clearly wasn't mine to fix, and I let it go. It's still painful—cutting ties with anyone close always is. But I learned a powerful lesson. We do not owe our presence to people who drain our life force.

When you change, it forces others to reexamine their own choices, which can be uncomfortable for them. They may unconsciously try to pull you back into familiar patterns because it makes them feel safer, or they may worry that when you make changes it will leave them behind. Remember that their resistance isn't always about you. It's often about their own fears, discomfort, or unexamined beliefs.

When others push back, it's important to stay grounded in your why. Why is this shift necessary? What will it allow you to do, feel, or become? How does this decision bring you closer to your core values? What will staying in this state of violation cost you in the long run? People resist what they don't understand. You don't need their permission to change, but offering insight into *why* you're changing can help others understand and support you. This is a good time to revisit the Head-Heart-Core exercise (chapter 3) as a tool to communicate your truth with clarity and kindness.

Of course, not everyone will get it—and that's okay. It's not your burden to carry. Some relationships will evolve with you; others may fade. And some people will resist at first but eventually come around when they see you thriving. The key is to trust yourself more than you fear disappointing others. In the end, it will be worth it. Your life belongs to you.

TAKEAWAYS

- Violations may seem petty on the surface, but the reason they're so frustrating is that they go against who we are at our core. Violations are emotional clues—moments when your environment or relationships clash with your human operating system. Far from being just annoyances, they reveal what matters most to you and can become powerful tools for growth if approached with curiosity rather than judgment.

- Instead of reacting impulsively to emotional triggers, learn to name and understand violations so you can respond with clarity. Ask:

    a. **What exactly is the violation?** Identify the specific moment or detail that upset you. Pinpoint what, exactly, caused your mood or energy to shift.

b. **Why is this a violation of my operating system?** Ask why the moment felt like an attack on your values. Tie it back to your HOS to see how your inner compass is being disrupted.

c. **How is this my responsibility?** Explore how you may have contributed to the violation, even indirectly. Taking radical self-responsibility returns power to you and keeps you from blaming others unnecessarily.

d. **How can I reset my course?** Decide whether the external situation can be changed or if an internal shift (reframing, boundary setting, mindset) is necessary to regain alignment.

e. **What can I learn?** View the violation as a teacher. What does this reveal about you? What opportunity for growth, change, or deeper authenticity does it offer?

- Sometimes, violations are signs that something major needs to change. Recognizing violations and choosing alignment isn't always easy, especially when it means disappointing others or ending relationships, but it's important to stay steady on the course and rooted in your why.

CHAPTER 9

ASK GROUNDING QUESTIONS

If you've been doing the work as we go along, you've done something extraordinary. You've gathered the scattered pieces of your life and shaped them into a cohesive, powerful truth. It's not uncommon for people to describe this part of the process as a kind of awakening: like remembering something they've always known or finally seeing themselves clearly after years of blur.

Maybe you're feeling this deep sense of alignment yourself. The past makes more sense. Your quirks and patterns stop feeling random. You feel anchored in a way that's hard to put into words. Maybe you've felt that click of recognition, that soft exhale of "Yes. This is me." You're ready to head back out into the world, your new insight in tow.

But the real world doesn't pause just because you've had a breakthrough. Emails pile up. Kids get sick. Clients call. A friend sends a text with bad news and suddenly you're not operating from your truth—you're reacting from your habits.

If you've done any kind of self-development work before, you know this cycle. The incredible epiphanies we uncover in quiet moments feel rock solid at the time, but they slip away unless you consciously integrate them.

That's why this chapter is so important.

I don't want you to just uncover your operating system, come up with a Dig word, and go back to real life. The goal now is to live from this place, day in and day out. In this chapter and the next, we're going to build practical tools *specific to you* that help you anchor your Dig word and operating system into your everyday decisions, habits, and relationships. These tools are designed to help you handle situations in less reactive, more conscious ways. You'll be able to use them daily to energize yourself, to stay on course, to make decisions that are truly aligned, and to dust yourself off and get back in the saddle when things go awry.

And it all starts with a question.

ASKING GROUNDING QUESTIONS

The more you're living in your operating system, the more successful, ease-filled, flowy, and enjoyable life can become. Decisions come more easily. You more quickly tap into your wants and needs. You communicate with more clarity and confidence, which lets you make a bigger impact on the world around you.

Life won't magically become free of conflict or pain, of course. But when you're flowing with your operating system instead of trying to fight it, you'll have a much less frustrating time navigating the rapids you come across.

The problem is that it's extremely easy to float out of your operating system in the course of daily life. No matter how mind-blowing it was to remember your operating system, it's only human to forget it once life gets busy. We get caught up in external stressors and distractions that pull us away from our purpose and values. We get wrapped up in other people's expectations and hopes and desires and forget our own. We start being pulled off course by the currents of the world around us.

That's where grounding questions come in.

A grounding question is a recalibration tool. The purpose is to pull you back into your operating system when you have floated out, by acknowledging that your operating system is where you thrive and providing a path back to living in it. It's a simple, direct question that reminds us to return to our foundation so that we can act from a place of authenticity rather than reactivity.

You can use grounding questions:

- **When you feel disconnected from your purpose.** When life gets moving too fast, we sometimes lose touch with the things that truly matter. Your grounding question can act as a path back to what's important.
- **When you're triggered or stressed.** When you find yourself reacting rather than responding, your grounding question can break the cycle of reactivity and help you find clarity and make intentional choices.
- **When you have a major decision to make.** Whether it's accepting a new job, moving to a different city, or handling a difficult conversation, your grounding question is a way to frame tough choices through your operating system to figure out what is most aligned with you.
- **As part of your regular check-ins.** Even when things aren't going off the rails, grounding questions help keep us on course. Without regular check-ins, we drift. Writing your grounding question on a sticky note, setting it as a phone reminder, or using it as part of a morning ritual can help prevent that drift.

My Dig word is "Authentic." My operating system is all about finding your own frequency and being free to authentically express yourself with integrity and grace for the betterment of all. Whenever I'm acting in that operating system, I know I'm going to be okay—even if things aren't always turning out perfectly around me.

Whenever I'm feeling lost or out of alignment, I ask, "How real do you want to be?" The question opens up a whole spectrum of responses.

Sometimes I'll answer it with a number: "I want to be 2 percent real" or "I want to be 83 percent real." Sometimes I'll answer it as a statement: "I want to be very real" or "I'm not sure how much capacity I have to be real right now." Sure, my operating system wants me to be 100 percent real all the time. But in reality it doesn't always feel practical, and the way I answer this question lends me more information about how this situation is aligned with my operating system.

I might learn that I feel safe to fully show up as myself, or that I'm feeling strong enough to be real in an important situation, even though it might be tough. I might learn that I need to postpone or avoid the situation until I have the capacity to be more myself. After all, I have enough data points about my life by now to know that if my gut is telling me to tone down my "realness" in a certain moment, pushing through is not going to turn out well for anyone.

Whatever answer I give to my grounding question often leads to follow-up questions such as "What would it take for me to be real right now?"

The answer to that might be "Well, I haven't slept well for three nights, and I'm exhausted. I have no energy. I should probably have this meeting or address this situation tomorrow when I'm more refreshed." Or "I just had an argument with somebody, and I cannot deal with having any more conflict in my life. This situation isn't worth the stress of showing up in a way that I know will cause conflict, so I'm just going to be 2 percent real right now and let it go."

When I get to the heart of my reason for not wanting to be real, it uncovers next steps. Maybe I need to show myself some care and attention before I can enter into a place of authenticity. Maybe I just need to punt something down the line a little bit.

Sometimes you don't have the luxury to push something off when you can't fully show up for it, but most of the time you don't actually have to act or speak in that exact moment. Whether it's as small as taking a deep breath or an hour lunch break off-site, or as big as tabling a hard conversation for tomorrow or next week, you're allowed to take the space you need to collect yourself, get more centered, get more curious, get more spaciousness, or whatever it is you need for you to show up in a way that's aligned with your operating system. (Hint! It probably will involve asking your grounding question or taking one of your alignment actions, which we'll talk about next.)

Of course, sometimes I ask my grounding question and the answer is, "I want to be 100 percent real—let's go!" When that's the answer, things always turn out great. Even if the outcome doesn't turn out how I want, the fact that I showed up authentically brings me more into alignment with my operating system, which feels amazing. Being authentic is a much easier way to live than constantly holding yourself back, and I'm at my best when I'm willing to be fully authentic and present.

"How real do you want to be?" is the question that helps me show up as my best self, time and again—but every Dig word and operating system will have their own version.

Let's take a look at my client Jim Miller as another example. Jim is a badass. He's a veteran who spent his career in national security, working in high-pressure environments where people's lives are on the line. You'd expect his Dig word to be something like "Strength" or "Discipline" or "Protect"—but instead, it's "Love." His entire leadership philosophy is to meet people from a place of love, so he's always asking, "How can I approach this with love?"

This question helps keep him in his operating system, where he's most able to lead effectively, especially in high-stakes situations. It keeps him from slipping into fear, control, or rigidity in tough moments—states that are antithetical to his operating system and Dig word.

That said, your grounding question doesn't have to contain your Dig word. Jim's and my words fit well into a grounding question, but some people find their Dig word somewhat triggering. After all, a Dig word encompasses both our superpower and our shadow—the thing that drives us and the thing we struggle with most.

For example, I recently Dug someone whose word is "Possibility." We knew we'd landed on the right word when she said, "Possibility is what excites me! But it's also my Achilles' heel. I can get very overwhelmed by possibilities and stall out."

When I suggested *"What is possible here?"* as her grounding question, she balked and said, "That would overwhelm me even more!" Imagining more possibility when she was already stressed out didn't ground her—it made her spiral.

Instead, we found another critical word from her operating system, "choose," and crafted a question that helped cut through an overwhelming number of possibilities and land in the present moment. Her grounding question became *"What choice do I need to make?"*

Your grounding question doesn't even need to be a question. Another client, Dr. Mark McBride-Wright, is a leader in diversity and inclusion, focusing on psychological safety in the engineering industry. His Dig word is "Justice," and that is the basis for his work in helping companies cultivate inclusive, thriving cultures.

During his Dig, we started out by playing with questions like *"Where is the injustice?"* or *"What feels just in this moment?"* The problem was that the word "Justice" was very triggering to Mark. Just thinking about injustice would send him into fight mode. He'd get reactive, angry, and frustrated—none of which grounded him in a way that actually created the shift he wanted.

Instead, we landed on a grounding statement rather than a question: *"Just breathe."*

For Mark, doing justice work isn't about being in a constant battle—it's about staying present, making strategic choices, and keeping his energy for the long game. His grounding statement reminds him to pause, take a breath, and respond instead of react.

A grounding question is essentially what we really need to hear in our most trying moments. When we're triggered, angry, stressed-out, or frustrated, or when we just need a moment of clarity. These are the moments when we really need to be tapping into our operating systems, and a grounding question is the fastest, most direct way to get there.

CRAFTING YOUR GROUNDING QUESTION

Now it's time to craft a question of your own. Start with your Dig word and try to craft a question that uses it (or a synonym, like "authentic" and "real"). If your Dig word is too triggering and sends you into fight or flight, explore the rest of your operating system to see if another word helps bring you back down to the ground. Finally, if a question doesn't feel right, play with a statement that could help ground you.

Remember, your grounding question doesn't have to have anything to do with your Dig word, if that doesn't feel right. It just needs to provide a doorway back into your operating system in a way that gives you a clear answer for moving forward.

When crafting a grounding question, remember that the best ones are short, direct, and expansive.

Short. Your grounding question should be simple and easy to ask. This is especially important when you're asking this question in a stressful moment—you don't need the additional complication of navigating a long, complex question. Sometimes I'll say, "Ask a question that a nine-year-old could understand." When your brain is managing too much, that's about all the capability it has.

Direct. If you want a direct answer, you need to ask a direct question. This is especially true when it comes to grounding questions! Don't leave yourself a bunch of room to be wishy-washy in your responses. Craft a question that gets to the heart of what you need to know.

Expansive. You don't want a question that can be answered with a simple yes or no—you want something that serves as the beginning of an interaction with yourself. Think of it as opening the door into the self-awareness and self-expression that are necessary for you to be in your truth.

Like all the other work we've done in this book so far, don't worry about perfection here. You don't have to get the question or statement right on the first try. Here are some examples to get your creative juices flowing:

Self-Expression and Authenticity

- How real do I want to be right now?

- What truth needs to be spoken?

- Am I honoring my voice?

- What would it take to show up fully as myself?
- What part of me is trying to be expressed?
- Just be present.

Courage and Boldness

- What is the brave thing to do right now?
- Where am I playing small?
- What's one bold action I can take?
- How can I choose courage over comfort?
- What fear can I face in this moment?
- Stay the course.

Clarity and Focus

- What actually matters most right now?
- What choice do I need to make?
- What is the simplest next step?
- What can I let go of?
- What is my biggest priority?
- What's in my control?
- One thing at a time.

Freedom and Possibility

- Where can I find more ease?
- What are the possibilities?
- What would freedom feel like?
- How can I create momentum?

- Where am I feeling stuck?
- What is holding me back?
- Take the first step.
- Enjoy the moment.

Connection and Relationships

- How can I deepen my connection in this moment?
- What does love look like?
- What would lead to understanding?
- Where can I be of service?
- Walk in love.

Joy and Gratitude

- What am I grateful for?
- How can I bring more joy into my day?
- What's one thing that made me smile today?
- How can I shine my light?
- What sounds fun?
- Always seek the light!

Presence and Peace

- What is happening in this present moment?
- What do I need to release?
- What do I notice in the room around me?
- What do I feel in my body?
- Just breathe.

A DOORWAY HOME

When I'm with people close to me and we're trying to make a decision, I like to propose a game called First Reaction. It's simple. The only rule is that you have to immediately say your first reaction to whatever the question is.

If I ask, "Where do you want to go for dinner?" and invoke the First Reaction game, it means stop worrying about everything else: what I want, what the budget is, what we had for dinner last night, and so on. If your answer is "sushi," the game allows you to say that without worrying about whether that's the "right" decision or whether you're being accommodating enough, or frugal enough, or anything else.

You can say, "Hey, this is my first reaction. It's not thought through, but it's my unfiltered response."

In playing this game, I've found that in most cases, the first reaction is the right choice. You can reserve the right to change your mind or alter your opinion, but the first reaction is often the truest. And if we follow that course, everyone's usually pretty happy about it.

The choice of what to have for dinner is a low-stakes one, but it's an illustration of the role overthinking plays in our inauthenticity. If you're the kind of heady, intellectual person who tends to worry about what everyone else wants and overthink decisions, First Reaction is a shortcut through all that. It allows you to speak your wants without watering them down or anticipating what everybody else needs.

A grounding question should serve the same purpose.

Think of a grounding question like a compass. No matter how lost or disoriented you might feel, this question helps you reorient yourself to your true north. Whether you're navigating a stressful situation, debating a career move, or simply needing a moment of clarity in a chaotic day, asking yourself the right grounding question can make all the difference.

Some people use their grounding question as a prompt to go in a direction that's most true for them. Other people use it more like a litmus test, allowing them to try on answers and feel where they hit on their Resonance Meter.

Like everything else in this book, though, the answer to a grounding question won't be binary, or black-and-white. Instead, it offers us guidance. Insight into what the right path is for us. A doorway back home into our operating system.

Eventually, I've found that it becomes more of a reminder. At this point, I've asked myself *"How real do you want to be?"* so many times that I no longer have to spend much time on the answer. Because by this stage, I know it's always going to turn out better for me if I show up with 100 percent authenticity—internally, at least. Externally, it might not always line up with what I was hoping for, but I've accepted that this is just part of my life path. I might as well sink into it.

What reminder do you need?

TAKEAWAYS

- A grounding question is a personal go-to phrase that reconnects you to your operating system when you're stressed, reactive, or drifting off course. Grounding questions are useful in a variety of moments: when you feel disconnected from your purpose, when you're triggered or overwhelmed, when you face a big decision, as part of a daily check-in or ritual.

- Your grounding question should be:
    - **Short:** easy to remember and say in stressful moments.
    - **Direct:** cuts to the heart of what you need to know.
    - **Expansive:** prompts meaningful reflection or a path forward.

- For some, the Dig word itself is a great focal point (*"How can I approach this with love?"*). For others, the word may be too triggering, and another part of their operating system works better (*"What choice do I need to make?"*). Grounding statements like *"Just breathe"* can work better for some people, especially when questions trigger anxiety or frustration.

- A good grounding question is like a compass. It reorients you when you're off track, helping you pause, reset, and move forward from a place of authenticity and alignment. It helps you learn to trust your gut. Your first response to your grounding question is often your most aligned one. You can adjust later, but start by honoring what you know deep down.

- Eventually, it becomes second nature. Over time, asking your grounding question builds a habit of self-awareness and alignment. It becomes a gentle, constant reminder of who you really are.

CHAPTER 10

LIVING AN ALIGNED LIFE

You know that feeling when things just aren't quite working?

Maybe it's just one of those days where you're constantly off-kilter. Maybe for weeks now, you've had this uneasy, sinking feeling every time you walked through the doors to your office or sat down at your desk to work. Maybe this has gone on so long that merely waking up and getting out of bed has become an insurmountable chore.

When you're out of alignment, things feel hard. Draining. You feel stuck, resentful, or unmotivated—like you're swimming against the current, but you're not even sure why. It's easy to get bumped out of alignment for a short time or, unfortunately, to get stuck in it for months or years.

Sometimes, the source of misalignment is abundantly clear. An important relationship has become full of conflict and strife. A job you thought you'd love has turned out to be a massive source of stress. The place you live is starting to feel like a prison where you can't fully express yourself.

But other times, the misalignment might just seem like a slight annoyance. Like a coworker who gets on your nerves, a squeaky door hinge that you keep meaning to do something about, or an important task that—for some reason—you just keep procrastinating on.

Small misalignments can seem like no big deal. But have you ever driven a car that's just a bit out of alignment? It's not dangerous. The car is still drivable. Still, it's frustrating when the wheels are always tugging slightly to the left or right—and it requires more effort from you to keep it on course. It's worth addressing this misalignment sooner rather than later, because it can become more than a minor annoyance; it can put a serious amount of strain on your vehicle over time.

Just like driving that car, living out of alignment might work for a while. You can convince yourself to stay in a job that drains you, a relationship that feels wrong, or a lifestyle that doesn't match your values. You might even become really good at it, going through the motions and checking all the boxes to make it look like everything is fine. But it's not sustainable. Over time, the wear and tear starts to show. The ride gets bumpier. The car becomes harder to control—and eventually, something breaks.

I learned this the hard way through my divorce.

By all accounts, my marriage looked fine. But deep down, I knew something was wrong. For years, I ignored the feeling. I told myself the discomfort I was experiencing wasn't a big deal, and certainly not worth upending my life over. But the misalignment didn't go away. It just got louder, until it was a persistent, all-consuming anxiety. That constant anxiety was a quiet—or sometimes not-so-quiet— signal from my core saying that I wasn't living in my own truth.

When I finally made the decision to leave my marriage, everything shifted. It wasn't easy. In fact, life got exponentially harder in the short term. But something surprising happened: My anxiety almost completely disappeared. Even though the path I was on became more challenging, it was *my* path. It felt true. And that truth created a kind of peace I hadn't felt in years.

When Jolene Park first came to me, she was already a successful corporate wellness consultant and trainer. She had built a solid reputation teaching people how to live healthier lives—taking a comprehensive approach to nutrition, movement, and stress management. From the outside, her career looked clear and aligned.

But she had a nagging feeling that she'd been put here to do something. As we went through the Dig, she started to realize that her bigger why had to do with helping people vitalize themselves on every possible level—physically, mentally, emotionally, spiritually.

Her word, "Nourish," gave Jolene language for something she'd been feeling all along. It also gave her clarity to make a major personal decision: to stop drinking alcohol. Not because she hit rock bottom or because she wanted to wear a badge of sobriety—but because alcohol didn't nourish her. It depleted her and wasn't congruent with her work in optimizing personal and corporate wellness.

She gave a TEDx Talk on the topic of Gray Area Drinking, the kind of drinking that affects countless people who don't fit the traditional label of "alcoholic" but are questioning their relationship with alcohol. Jolene spoke not as someone issuing a warning but as someone offering an invitation. Since then, she's built a global coaching and training community and become a pioneering authority on Gray Area Drinking. Now, she teaches others how to reclaim their energy, clarity, and well-being—without shame or labels—when they quit drinking, not because they have to, but because they want to.

The reality is, you can't fake alignment forever—and things rarely shift back into alignment on their own. If you're out of sync with your truth, your body, mind, or spirit will eventually demand your attention. And when that happens, you're faced with a choice: keep pushing forward on a path that doesn't serve you, or stop to recalibrate and realign with who you really are.

Once you see the truth, it can be very hard to unsee it. By now, you're probably starting to notice more than a few places in your life that are out of alignment with your operating system. Are you willing to do what it takes to get back on track?

Believe me, it's worth it. Jolene's story is a perfect example of how living in alignment with your Dig word not only lifts you up but can elevate others as well. If you've got that nagging feeling that something's missing or that you could be showing up more fully, it's time to check your alignment.

In this chapter, we're going to talk about what to do when you feel out of alignment—either with the world around you or with other important people in your life. We're bringing it back to the conversation about frequencies that we had in chapter 2. Only now, instead of just learning to recognize frequencies in your life, we're going to talk about how to shift them.

It starts with paying attention to where things feel off.

YOUR ALIGNMENT MAP

Picture a weather map with layers for precipitation, wind speed and direction, temperature, humidity, air-quality index, and more. The weather reporter can toggle all these different layers off and on to get a more in-depth view of how the weather patterns are going to affect the local region. Is it going to be a good day for a bike ride with friends? Do you need to pull your warmest hat out of storage or find your umbrella?

I like to think of alignment in a similar way. Each of us has key layers—different areas in our lives—that might be more or less in alignment. Much like a weather map that shows storms forming before they hit, an Alignment Map helps you spot problem areas before they turn into full-blown crises. It gives you a big-picture view of your life, helping you make intentional shifts instead of staying stuck in harmful patterns.

There are four major categories we track:

1. **Purpose:** How aligned do you feel with your work, mission, spirituality, or creative expression?
2. **Community:** Do your personal and professional relationships feel supportive and nourishing?
3. **Health:** Is your physical, mental, and emotional well-being in balance?
4. **Finances:** Is your financial situation supporting or restricting your ability to live in alignment?

Each of these areas impacts the others, and if one is way off, it can throw everything else into chaos. For example, life may be all sunshine and warm breezes in your community and work, but if your health is suffering, storm clouds will brew over your relationships and work performance, too. If your finances are stuck in cloudy conditions, it'll start to rain on your friendships and impact your health.

You don't need a fancy app or green screen to make an Alignment Map. You just need a simple system for checking in with yourself. (For a printable Alignment Map, go to erinweed.com/justoneword.)

1. **Draw Four Circles:** Label them Purpose, Community, Health, and Finances.
2. **Rate Each Area:** On a scale of 1 to 10, how aligned do you feel in each area? (1 is completely off track, drained, and frustrated; 10 is fully aligned and fulfilled.)
3. **Identify Misalignment:** Go through the exercise that follows to explore where you feel the biggest struggle or

resistance. Go with your gut here—it's probably been trying to tell you about this misalignment for a while.

4. **Take One Alignment Action:** Choose one thing to do this week to bring a low-scoring area closer to alignment.

We'll talk about taking alignment actions in a second, but first let's peel back those layers and pinpoint the source of the misalignment.

Start by getting curious and asking yourself some questions. Grab your journal and begin freewriting, if that works well for you. Go for a walk and have a mental dialogue with yourself (or a verbal one). You could also enlist the help of a friend who's a good listener and ask them to be your sounding board.

This is also a great time to go back to the Head-Heart-Core exercise in chapter 3 and check in with those three aspects of your truth.

Let's say your purpose area is feeling like a 3 or 4 lately—maybe you've woken up for several weeks in a row with a deep dread of going to work. Start asking yourself why, and continue to ask why until you've reached an answer that hits high on your Resonance Meter.

- Is it the work itself? Why? (Maybe it's not aligned with your purpose.)
- Is it the people? Why? (Maybe you feel disconnected or undervalued.)
- Is it the schedule? Why? (Maybe your need for freedom is being stifled.)
- Is it the environment? Why? (Maybe it drains your energy or creativity.)
- Is it *you*? Why? (Maybe you've outgrown this job but you're scared to admit it.)

As you delve deeper into the why behind your feeling, you'll get to the core of where your work is out of sync with your operating system. And, most importantly, it becomes something you can take action on—even if it's just making small shifts to improve things.

Do this in every category of your Alignment Map where you gave yourself a low score.

Maybe you'll realize your purpose score is low because your work no longer excites you. Your community score might be low because you've been neglecting friendships. Your health score might be low because you're fighting off a cold or you haven't been sleeping well. Your finance score might be low because you were hit with an unexpected tax bill or took a pay cut.

Now, instead of feeling generally *off* in your life but not knowing why, you have clarity. You might realize that your life isn't actually falling apart—you just need to catch up on sleep or stop avoiding a hard conversation with a friend. Or you might realize that you've been grinning and bearing your way through each day, but your map shows a major storm on the horizon and it's time for a significant change.

Either way, gaining clarity with your Alignment Map allows you to take action before the misalignment gets even worse.

TAKING ALIGNMENT ACTIONS

All right. What do you *do* when things are out of alignment? While grounding questions help you recenter in the moment, alignment actions are the steps that help sync your life back up with your unique operating system.

They can be small habits that help you live more of your life in the flow, like keeping a gratitude journal or meditating. They can be bigger steps that course-correct situations, like having a hard conversation with a loved one or renovating your home to make it feel more like a place you want to spend time. And they can be big, bold leaps like quitting your job and moving across the country to follow that dream that's been whispering to you for years.

Because everyone's operating system and Dig word are so different, there's no one-size-fits-all solution to get you back on track. Just like one person's grounding question might cause another person to spiral, each person's alignment actions will be unique to their personality and values. You'll need to discover the ones that are most effective for you.

There are three types of alignment actions you can take:

1. The Small, Simple Shift

What's one tiny thing you could do today to feel better about this situation? These are quick, easy actions that immediately bring a little more alignment into your life. They might not fix everything, but they move you in the right direction and can help build momentum because they're fairly low stakes and simple to implement.

- **Purpose:** You realize you've been feeling stuck in your work because it's not using your creativity in the way you'd like. A small alignment action might be setting aside thirty minutes today for your own creative work.
- **Community:** You realize you're feeling lonely because you've grown apart from old friends and haven't made many new ones in your current phase of life. A small alignment action might be calling an old friend you wish you spoke with more, or even just texting them to set up a time to talk.
- **Health:** You realize you've been sleeping poorly for weeks now, and it's starting to cascade into other parts of your

health. A small alignment action might be taking a quick catnap to refresh your energy this afternoon or going to bed early tonight.

- **Finances:** You realize that your debts have snowballed to a place where they're starting to be a serious point of stress for you. A small alignment action might be logging on to pay a past-due bill or canceling a subscription you've been meaning to cut for a while.

2. The Hard but Necessary Action

Sometimes, alignment requires a bigger shift—one that might feel uncomfortable in the moment but is necessary for long-term well-being. These are more forceful actions that require more effort to undertake but create more lasting change. They can also provide more mental relief, especially if it means taking care of something that's been on your mind for a while.

- **Purpose:** If you want to use your creativity more at work, a hard but necessary action might be to pitch your boss on a project that showcases your skills and might lead to being more aligned at work overall.
- **Community:** If you're feeling disconnected and lonely, a hard but necessary action might be to sign up for a class where you could meet new people in your area who share your interests.
- **Health:** If you've been sleeping poorly for a while, a hard but necessary action might be to make changes to your bedtime routine (like reducing screen time or alcohol) that will help you unwind and relax more.
- **Finances:** If your debts have snowballed, a hard but necessary action might be to sit down and take a good look

at your spending, then set a firm budget for yourself and cancel your credit card.

3. The Big, Bold Leap

There are times when alignment requires a massive change—the kind that shakes up your whole life but ultimately leads to deeper fulfillment. One of my favorite examples comes from my client James. His Dig word is "Explore," which was out of alignment with his predictable daily life. When I asked him what big, bold change he could make, he lit up and said, "Go to Burning Man!"

You guessed it: James bought a ticket to this freedom-loving, psychedelic-laden week in the desert. His wife, a friend of mine, later called me and (somewhat) jokingly said, "Erin, what have you done?" But that one decision cracked open a whole new world for him—leading him to study permaculture, shift careers, and create a more adventurous life that both he *and* his wife find fulfilling.

- **Purpose:** Maybe it's time to leave your noncreative job behind and return to school to do what you truly love.
- **Community:** Maybe a major lifestyle shift is required to connect you with the people you want to spend time with—you might need to move to a different town, quit hanging out with people who promote negative habits for you, or organize an event of your own that attracts the people you want in your life.
- **Health:** Maybe it's time to see a doctor about your sleep or address the relationship, job, or financial stressor that's keeping you up at night.
- **Finances:** Maybe you need to hire a financial coach, sell your expensive car, or downsize your home so you can live a more fulfilled life within your means.

To create your own alignment actions, take a look at your Alignment Map and identify what feels off. Then describe what alignment would look like. If this part of your life felt good, what would be different?

Finally, brainstorm one action in each category:

1. A small, simple shift (What could you do today?)
2. A hard but necessary step (What's one step that feels uncomfortable but needed?)
3. A big, bold leap (If you were fearless, what would you do?)

SETTING YOUR COURSE:
THE WORD-OF-THE-WEEK PRACTICE

My client Shawn is a landscape architect in California with an incredible gift for working with the natural world. His operating system revolves around regeneration and repurposing, and his approach to his work is that he doesn't just build—he transforms. Whether that means busting up a big block of cement in a client's yard to reuse as a retaining wall or turning old concrete pavers into a waterfall fountain, Shawn's goal is to reduce waste by taking what's already there and turning it into something extraordinary.

It was no surprise that his Dig word turned out to be "Conscious." Everything about his work and life resonates with a deep awareness of the interconnectedness of people and nature. Every week, he sends out a gratitude newsletter to friends and family, where he shares what he's grateful for, and I look forward to that email every week.

Then, in early 2025, tragedy struck. Shawn's home was destroyed in the California wildfires that ravaged Los Angeles and the surrounding areas. The loss he faced was staggering. It wasn't just the physical structure of his home, but the memories, the security, and the sense of self his home represented.

The day after I learned about Shawn's home being destroyed, I remember thinking to myself that he probably wasn't going to send a gratitude email that week. He'd need a break—and I couldn't imagine he had much to feel grateful for. But, sure enough, Shawn's weekly email showed up in my inbox. I was bracing myself for the grief and despair I knew he must be feeling, but Shawn's email floored me. Despite everything, he still had a long list of things to be grateful for.

He was leaning into his Dig word. He was choosing to approach this unimaginable situation with consciousness, staying present with both the pain and the possibility of what could come next.

One thing in particular stood out to me. Shawn's office, which was separate from the house, survived the fire. On the side of the garage, there's a mural with the words "You Are Enough"—and those words remained untouched by the flames.

Words are powerful. And Shawn's story shows that, no matter what challenges life throws your way, your human operating system and Dig word can be your guide and a touchstone for navigating the unknown. Shawn's alignment with his purpose allowed him to stay present, focus on gratitude, and consciously choose his next steps instead of being consumed by fear or anger.

Assessing your alignment helps you identify where things feel off. Alignment actions help you get back on course. And having a regular practice—like Shawn's gratitude email—keeps you on course when things get difficult.

One of my favorite practices for staying aligned with your operating system is the word of the week. It's as simple as it sounds, but it can be extremely powerful.

Here's how it works. Each week, I pick one word that represents the energy, intention, or focus I want to bring into my life. This word doesn't override my Dig word. Instead, it complements it. Some weeks, my word is practical—if I feel like I've gotten stuck in my own head and need to pay more attention to the world outside, I might choose "notice." Other times, it's more abstract, like "shibumi" (a Japanese concept of effortless mastery).

There are a few different factors that go into choosing a word. I ask:

- What's on my calendar for the week?
- What will I be navigating emotionally?
- What do I want to learn about this week?
- What challenges am I facing?
- How do I want to affect the people around me?

I always start with my operating system and grounding question. For example, maybe I want my word of the week to be "inspire." Sounds great, right? But when I ask my grounding question—"How real do I want to be?"—I might realize I'm not fully in a place where I can inspire right now. When I keep asking why, I might find that I'm running on empty after weeks on the go. With that information in mind, I might instead choose a word of the week like "rest" or "recharge."

You might start by looking at your current challenges and do a quick check on your Alignment Map. What's been coming up for you lately? Are you feeling overwhelmed, disconnected, or stuck? Do you need more focus, patience, courage, or creativity?

Next, ask your grounding question to get more clarity in the moment.

Finally, pick a word that helps you shift toward alignment. If you've been feeling chaotic, maybe your word is "steady" or "foundation." If you've been procrastinating, maybe your word is "action" or "choose." The right word will feel expansive, like it's opening up a possibility for you.

Once you've chosen your word, write it somewhere you'll see it often—in your planner, on a sticky note, or as your phone's lock screen. Throughout the week, keep checking in with your word. Set an intention each morning to embody your word. Use it to reframe your responses when challenges arise throughout the day. In your reflections, consider how your word impacted you throughout the day.

If this appeals to you, you can expand this practice into greater time frames. I'm not a big fan of New Year's resolutions, but I *love* choosing a word of the year! For example, in 2025, my word was "chisel," inspired by the great artists who chisel masterpieces out of marble by carving away everything that doesn't belong in the statue. I realized that if I want to live my most authentic life, I need to focus on cutting away that which no longer serves me and focus on leaning into the goodness that's already in my life.

The beauty of this practice is that it allows you to consciously direct your energy toward what you need most without a ton of time or effort. Over time, it creates a rhythm of intentional living and helps you stay aligned with your operating system and Dig word instead of reacting to whatever life throws your way.

ALIGNED RELATIONSHIPS

I already told you I've never met two people with the exact same human operating system. In fact, I don't think it's possible. Our operating systems are as unique as fingerprints, shaped by our stories, experiences, and Core truths. But what I've learned is that some frequencies are deeply complementary. When you overlay them, they enhance each other and play off each other in unique ways.

Think of it like music: two different instruments playing in harmony. Alone, each one has its own distinct sound, but together, they create something richer and more complex.

When you understand your own human operating system, you don't just learn how you operate on your own. You also gain a deep understanding of how your operating system interacts with and complements the most important people in your life. And when you recognize those frequencies and find ways to align them, it can be extremely powerful.

Relationships, at their core, have their own frequency. Every connection—romantic, professional, or personal—has a unique rhythm, an underlying current that dictates how the two people interact, support each other, and clash. And just like an individual's operating system, a relationship's frequency isn't random. It's a force that's been there all along, shaping the dynamic between people, whether they recognize it or not.

In addition to individuals, I've been hired to Dig duos as well. Romantic relationships, family connections, and business partnerships can also benefit when you understand the shared frequency you have with your partner. Their frequency illuminates what drives someone, what scares them, and what fuels them.

This is the power of naming a relationship's Dig word. It's not about changing the people in it—it's about bringing clarity to the unseen energy that exists between them. It can also help you understand when those relationships shift.

For example, I've recently been feeling a shift in one of my closest friendships. For over a decade, this person has been a constant in my life. We've supported each other through massive transitions, personal growth, career changes, and everything in between. The energy between us had always been strong, but lately, things have felt…different. Plans take more effort. Conversations don't flow as easily. There's a sense that we're not quite landing in the same place anymore.

Nothing specific happened. We didn't have a falling-out. There was no betrayal, just a subtle shift.

At first, my instinct was to fix it. To analyze what had changed and reach for ways I could make things feel like they used to. But the more I sat with it, the more I realized maybe this wasn't something I needed to fix. Maybe the frequency that once connected us was "healing," and once that happened, our connection had served its purpose.

It's okay for our connections to be complete or get transformed into something new. For my friend and me, that means loosening our grip on the past and making space for whatever this next phase looks like. Maybe we'll realign in a new way. Maybe we'll drift apart. Either way, I know our connection wasn't wasted. It was real, it was meaningful, and it shaped us both.

Not every frequency is meant to last forever in the same form. And that's okay. Because honoring the truth of a relationship—whether that means deepening it, reshaping it, or letting it go—is the greatest act of respect we can give it.

TAKEAWAYS

- Misalignment shows up when life feels hard, draining, or stuck. It can be obvious (like a toxic relationship) or subtle (like low-grade daily anxiety), but either way, it wears you down over time. Left unaddressed, small frustrations build into bigger problems, just like a car slightly out of alignment eventually suffers serious wear and tear.
- Use an Alignment Map to help see where you're off track. Check in regularly with four key areas: purpose, community, health, and finances. Rate each area, and identify where you're most misaligned.
- Once you name where you're feeling misaligned and why, you can choose alignment actions that bring you closer to your truth.
- There are three types of alignment actions:
  - **Small, simple shifts** (quick, easy adjustments you can make today)
  - **Hard but necessary actions** (bigger, slightly uncomfortable changes for lasting improvement)
  - **Big, bold leaps** (major life shifts that create deep realignment)
- You can stay aligned over time with a word-of-the-week practice. Choose a word each week (based on your needs and challenges) to help you consciously live in tune with your human operating system.
- Every close connection—whether personal, romantic, or professional—creates its own dynamic frequency. Some frequencies strengthen you, some shift, and some eventually need to be released. Honor the truth of each relationship. Sometimes the most aligned act is to deepen the connection; other times, it's to let it change or end with grace.

CHAPTER 11

YOUR PURPOSE IS YOUR MESSAGE

Sometimes we find our purpose at the top of a proverbial mounstaintop while doing deep, formal self-work. Sometimes we find it in a bar while having whiskey with friends.

A year or so ago, my good friend (and Dig client) Ryan invited me out for a drink. He brought along his neighbor, Greg, who had recently been laid off from a corporate sales job. Greg was one of those successful suburban dads who was clearly at a crossroads. He'd worked hard, he was smart, he was good with people—but it was pretty clear he wasn't sure what was next in life.

As the conversation turned to what he was into and what was important to him, my Dig spidey sense started tingling. Greg wasn't asking for a session, but I can't help it when my internal antenna goes up. I started to feel into his frequency.

I kept sensing that he held all these realities within him, each with its own level of truth, and that he had an exceptional ability to wander in the space between them. He had a quiet gift for holding seemingly contradictory things at once. I reflected this back to him and told him I felt a clear sense of duality. Greg connected with the idea of "Duality" being his Dig word right away—but we didn't spend too much more time on it. After all, this was just a casual night.

I didn't think about it again until Greg emailed me a few months later. He wanted me to be one of the first people to know he'd decided not to go back to corporate America. Instead, he was opening a coffee roaster. And what did he name it? Duality Coffee.

Of course.

He told me our conversation made him realize he didn't want to go back to corporate life. He wanted to create something slower, more intentional. A space for people to gather, reflect, and talk about the mysteries of life—over a damn fine cup of coffee.

Greg's story is proof that tapping into your purpose doesn't just help you establish alignment internally. Instead, giving yourself permission to pursue that purpose has a tendency to shine out into the world.

Your purpose becomes your message.

When Greg embraced the word "Duality," it didn't just give him a framework to understand himself—it also gave him a brand and a mission. Even if customers never hear the story behind the name, they'll feel the energy and enthusiasm in the finished product. They'll get a taste of that expansiveness and mystery and carry it with them out through the rest of their day.

Until now, we've been working on finding clarity around who you are and what you're here to do. Now we're going to talk about infusing that purpose into your message so it rings out loud and clear into the world.

Don't worry. I'm not asking you to run out tomorrow and give a TEDx Talk or write a book. You don't have to start a business and name it after your Dig word, like Greg did. Living out your message can look like a vulnerable conversation with your kid. It can be a moment of presence in a difficult meeting. It can be a story you share over tea with a neighbor, or in an Instagram post with the world.

But however you choose to share it, I'm convinced that you'll want to. So we're going to explore different ways in which you can apply your Dig word and your manifesto in the way you communicate, no matter who—or how big—your audience is.

One thing I've seen over and over is that when people find their purpose, it explodes out of them. Something about the discovery propels them into action. It's almost like once they find their purpose, they realize they've been running with weights around their ankles or driving with the parking brake on. The discovery dissolves those weights, releases that parking brake, and lets them live life at full throttle—whatever that means to them.

The truth is, once you remember who you really are and how you operate, it's almost harder *not* to express it. Because I specialize in helping people craft speeches, many of my clients already plan to express their purpose. But I've also seen so many people like Greg, who think they're just looking for personal insight and end up starting businesses, writing essays, changing careers, or launching new creative projects.

Take Damon, for example. His Dig word is "Nonconformity," and as the director of an art gallery that exhibits works by artists who have disabilities, he creates opportunities for people to express themselves in ways that don't conform to society's view of artists. But when his mother was diagnosed with Alzheimer's, Damon's drive for nonconformity caused him to start a program that simply wouldn't occur to most people: He handed a group of seniors with Alzheimer's cans of spray paint and taught them how to do graffiti.

People living with Alzheimer's spend so much of their life trying to remember the past. But graffiti? They'd never done that before. It completely removed the pressure to recall the past and live up to prior expectations. All they had to do was create something new and fun in the moment.

And it worked—Damon's new graffiti artists found a sense of joy and self-expression they hadn't felt in years, and their caretakers had a chance to join them in an activity that was purely fun. Instead of patient and caretaker, they became two people connecting over something joyful.

Whether you express your purpose through a manifesto taped to your wall, a new creative project, or simply the way you move through your day, what matters most is that you don't keep it locked inside. The world needs your message. And so do you.

FIRING UP THE THREE C'S WITH PURPOSE

Remember the Three C's we talked about in chapter 1? The first— epic *clarity* of purpose—allows you to communicate with *confidence*, which fuels your *connection* with your audience. Let's take a deeper look at some examples so you can see how this works on the other side of the Dig process.

Clarity

Brian Clark, founder of Copyblogger, was already a well-known name in the digital space when he came to me. He was a seasoned entrepreneur, sharp as hell, and deeply thoughtful about what was next for him. But, like so many people I've worked with, Brian had reached a transition point. He'd sold his company and he had a million ideas about what might come next—but he wasn't just looking to make money or fill his spare time. He wanted to find and pursue his purpose.

His Dig word ended up being "Further," and as we talked I could tell he was very tuned in to that frequency—especially as it related to his target audience. He and I are both Gen Xers, and he's always been interested in how our generation does things differently than the ones that came before. He was fascinated by questions like *"How could we go further in our approach to work?" "How could we go further in our approach to health?" "And, as we're all getting older, how can we go further in our approach to midlife, personal growth, and longevity?"*

Brian is a writer and blogger at heart, and even if he hadn't landed on this specific why, he probably would have started a great blog that addressed the topics of midlife, health, wealth, and so on. But instead, he started a newsletter called *Further*, where every essay is sharpened by this incredibly potent and relevant purpose.

"Further" captures how he thinks, how he creates, and how he wants to serve. By tapping into that frequency, he's able to communicate with epic clarity that has attracted an audience of over nineteen thousand subscribers. It doesn't matter if his audience is consciously aware of the word—they feel that drive and momentum.

Confidence

When you embrace your purpose, it becomes the energetic signature behind everything you create. And the clarity that comes from speaking from your operating system gives you built-in confidence and authority. People can tell that you're communicating from a place of deep truth, and *you* can tell, too.

Confidence gives you the strength to share your story, the strength to claim its power, and—in the case of my client Jennifer—the strength to transform it.

Jennifer Hopper was carrying a story most people couldn't begin to imagine. Years earlier, she'd survived a brutal home invasion where her partner was murdered and she herself was stabbed and barely escaped with her life. The story made national headlines and was turned into a book—and Jennifer found herself cast in a role she didn't want: "the survivor."

When she came to see me, she wasn't looking to rehash or heal her trauma. She was looking for a way to reframe her identity and understand her purpose so she could have the confidence to share it with others.

Her Dig word was "Space," and when it emerged it landed with quiet power. Her literal space—her home—had been violated. Her physical space had been scarred. Her emotional and mental space had been fractured. But "Space" didn't just describe what she'd lost; it revealed what she felt called to create for herself and others.

With newfound clarity of purpose, Jennifer understood her story wasn't just about the attack she had survived. It was about how we create space for healing. It was about her decades-long struggle with worth and giving herself permission to take up space in her own body. It was about designing physical spaces—beautiful, safe, intentional homes—that offer peace instead of pain.

Connection

Jennifer didn't want to be known forever as "the woman from that story." Getting clarity gave her the confidence to transform that story, creating space for herself and showing the rest of us how to do the same. It helped her see that she's not just a survivor. She's a guide. A space holder. A lighthouse. And in the process of creating space for herself, she's showing the rest of us how to do the same—and creating powerful connections with her community.

Because, as we discussed in chapter 1, connection is the inevitable outcome of clarity and confidence. When you speak from your truth, people are drawn to it. They might even be so drawn to it that they make you go viral in a way that blows YouTube's mind.

I met E. Napoletano when they were preparing to give a TEDx Talk. E. is a wildly fun person with a huge breadth of experience, and that was reflected in the talk they had already drafted. But honestly—and with much love to E.—the draft was all over the place.

I knew E. had the makings of a fantastic talk; we just needed to distill the chaotic draft down to a core message. So I started asking questions, jotting words on sticky notes, and going deeper and deeper until we'd arrived at a single word: "Permission."

Once we'd arrived at E.'s Dig word, we were able to lay the draft of their TEDx Talk over the top of that frequency. We made sure that the message was clear, that E. could deliver it with confidence, and that it connected with the audience.

Like, *really* connected. E.'s TEDx Talk, "Rethinking Unpopular," was ironically quite popular. Viral, even.

Of course, the talk doesn't center on the word "permission." E. didn't even use the word in the speech. But the word's frequency was infused in every sentence, just as it was infused in every aspect of E.'s life. Because this idea wasn't new to them. It was what they'd *always* been talking about, and how they'd *always* been living. E. gave themself permission to leave their successful branding career and move to Chicago to study comedy at Second City—and then to pivot again and study nursing. They gave themself permission to embrace their non-binary identity and live more fully in their truth.

If "permission" had been a gimmick to write a speech, E.'s TEDx Talk wouldn't have had a fraction of the impact that it did.

Which brings me to the biggest thing I want to make sure you take away from this book. The Dig isn't a party trick to help you sell more books or go viral. It's not a ploy that will help you convince people to see things your way or gain you fans and followers. We're talking about finding your purpose here. Your through line. Your truth.

And when you embrace that, it will be far more powerful than you can imagine.

YOUR MESSAGE ECOSYSTEM: HOW WILL YOUR MESSAGE SUSTAINABLY THRIVE?

Okay. Enough talk about how other people are using their purpose to bring their message to life. Let's get practical and talk about how *you* can do it, if that feels compelling. Because even if you never get up onstage or start a business or any of the other things my clients have done once they discovered their one word, in my experience, the more clarity people get around their purpose, the more they want to talk about it.

If that sounds like you, how can you imbue your purpose in every piece of your message—whether it's updating your website or giving a talk? How can you use your purpose to bring clarity to the multidimensional experience of your life? How do you carry your message into your work, your relationships, your creative projects, and your communication without diluting it?

If we look at a message as a living, breathing thing, then we also need to consider how to bring it into the world as something alive. It's like a house plant. If you suffocate it, depriving it of attention and light and water, it will shrivel up and die. If you nurture your message, though, it will thrive.

So let's start by shifting your perspective. It's time to get really clear about the ways that our message wants to thrive outside of us—sustainably.

First, I encourage you not to skip the manifesto step of the Dig. Or, if a manifesto doesn't feel right for you, find another way to summarize your purpose. If you're the sort of person who likes to read through without doing the exercises, that's fine. But please do that one sooner rather than later! With your manifesto (and epic clarity) in hand, you will have done that hard work of distilling big ideas down to a small number of words, and that is powerful!

Your message ecosystem is a visual, dynamic representation of how your purpose shows up in all the areas of your life. It gives you a high-level view of your work, energy, and impact—how you're showing up, where you're aligned, where you're off track, and where you might want to shift your focus.

In biology, an ecosystem is a network of interdependent organisms and systems, each one affecting the others. Your message ecosystem is no different. Your roles as an employee, entrepreneur, speaker, artist, or activist are all part of the same living system, with you—and your Dig word—at the center.

It's immensely helpful to create a visual representation of all these pieces of your ecosystem. Not only does it help you see all the places you're making an impact; it's a great tool for assessing what's going well, what's out of alignment, and how you could better allocate your finite attention and energy to get the biggest bang for your buck.

You might be tempted to skip this step and just go for it. Why worry so much about strategy? Just start sharing your story with reckless abandon and shouting your purpose from the rooftops with your speaking gigs, podcast, blog, book—the more the better, right?

Well, I know a girl who did just that. And let me tell you, she burned out hard.

(It's me! I'm talking about me.)

I ran full tilt during my Girls Fight Back years. I owned the business for twelve years, and my message ecosystem—which had grown organically without much thought or foresight—was all over the place. I was speaking at colleges, high schools, and corporations. I wrote a book that went through several editions. I was writing a monthly column in *CosmoGIRL!*

I was also traveling around two hundred days a year to give all these workshops, and when I was home I would conduct free pop-up workshops on the street. I had brought on corporate sponsors for my book tour, which came with a whole other layer of complexity. And, in the midst of all this, I thought it would be fun to open up a women's self-defense studio where I lived in Hoboken, New Jersey.

And it was really rad!

But I never stopped to think, "Hey, I'm traveling nonstop. What am I doing with a brick-and-mortar location?"

The Erin who was doing all these things had no idea how to slow down. She had no concept that she could get her message out in a way that didn't have to destroy her.

Because ultimately, after twelve years of running Girls Fight Back, my physical health was destroyed, I'd developed an anxiety disorder, and I wanted to crawl under a rock for a month and not come out.

When you're a public leader, when you've built your identity around helping others with your words, it's easy to forget there's a human behind the message. A human with limits. A human who needs rest. You.

I wish I could go back and tell that version of me: "You're allowed to do less. You're allowed to build smarter. You don't have to burn down your life to light the world."

These days, I do things differently.

Assessing your own message ecosystem doesn't have to be complicated. You can sketch it on a whiteboard or journal it out in a notebook. You can type it up in your notes app. Or, if you're feeling ambitious, you can design it digitally using a tool like Figma or Canva.

And by the way—your message doesn't need to go global in order for it to be successful. It can be a series of social media posts for your friends that documents your health journey, or a campaign speech that you craft while running for HOA president or a meaningful autobiography you write to share with your children someday. Words have impact, and the more authentic they are, the more change can happen.

Here's how to start:

1. Whatever medium you choose, put your name and Dig word in the center.

This is your sun, your energetic anchor. Everything else radiates from here.

2. Add the "bubbles" of your messaging around it.

Think of the roles, projects, platforms, and identities where you communicate or act from your purpose. This might include:

- Your full-time job
- A side hustle or creative project
- Public speaking or teaching
- Content creation
- Membership sites or communities
- Volunteer or community work
- Religious communities and social circles
- Your social media presence

Adjust the size of each bubble based on how much time or energy it takes up in your life. What portion of your day and percentage of your attention does your job take up? How about creating content? *Marketing* that content? How many hours (really) are you spending on your most creative work? How about on social media? How much time are you spending in various communities and social circles?

Notice that we're talking about time *and* energy. You might spend the most hours at a day job unrelated to your more purposeful work. But if it's a breeze, you enjoy yourself, and you don't have to take it home with you, it may feel like a small bubble, energetically.

Be honest with yourself—you're the only person who needs to see this.

3.   Break each bubble down.

Inside (or next to) each bubble, jot down the bullet points that make up that bubble. For example, list the specific social media platforms you use next to the social media bubble. Next to "content creation" you might list "blog," "newsletter," and anything else you create. If you take on volunteer projects or side hustles, list the different channels or income streams.

If you know the financials on these bullet points, it can be helpful to list those as well. How much do you earn from your paid newsletter? How much do you charge for individual consultations? How much income do you get from your day job? How much revenue do your online courses, books, speaking engagements, and other parts of your message ecosystem bring in?

I'm not implying that more money means better—there are many other ways to track how valuable a specific volunteer opportunity, community engagement, or social obligation is to your life. This is all just helpful intel as you're assessing your messaging.

4. Track what matters.

Finally, I like to add a series of symbols on each bubble to quickly note the boxes each bubble ticks. Draw:

- A heart for things you **love** doing
- A check mark for things that align with your **purpose**
- A dollar sign for things that bring in **money (or other value)**

Each of those are important considerations for your overall ecosystem. Ideally, a thriving message ecosystem has bubbles that contain all three—but that doesn't mean that every bubble needs to check all those boxes.

Maybe one of your bubbles is poetry, which gets a heart and a purpose check mark—but no dollar sign. You love writing poems and feel like they're strongly aligned with your purpose, but they're not paying the bills and that's probably okay.

Another bubble might be an online course you run, which gets a purpose check mark and a dollar sign—but no heart. You know this course is making a difference in people's lives, and it's providing a steady stream of income for you. But it's been a long time since you've been excited about it. And that might be okay, too.

A third bubble might just meet one of your three criteria. For me, social media only has a check mark. I don't love it and it doesn't make me money, but it does serve a higher purpose of getting my message out to people who need to hear it, and bringing them to other parts of my ecosystem.

On the other hand, my coaching bubble gets all three check marks. I love the work, it pays the bills, and helping companies create more authentic workplaces is *extremely* my jam.

5.   Reflect on each bubble's alignment.

Now that you have a clear picture of your message ecosystem, it's time to ask how aligned each bubble is with your Dig word, operating system, and purpose.

Ask yourself:

- Is this helping me spread my message?
- Does it energize me or drain me?
- Do I feel proud of how I show up here?
- Does this part of my life reflect my operating system?

Color in the bubbles to represent how aligned each bubble is with you—green for "thriving," yellow for "needs attention," red for "out of alignment."

This process can be extremely enlightening.

You might realize that your biggest, most time-consuming project is totally out of alignment with your purpose. Or that something small and quiet—a weekly writing practice, a monthly volunteer gig—feels the most true. You might notice that you're pouring energy into a space that isn't energizing you. Or that you've neglected a part of your ecosystem that wants to grow.

When I create these message ecosystems with clients, it often leads to clarity—not because they suddenly invent a new brand or message, but because they finally see the truth that's been there all along. They begin to rearrange their lives not around what they feel obligated to do but around what actually aligns with their purpose. This is what helps them get their message most clearly—and sustainably—to the people who need to hear it.

YOUR MESSAGE IS YOUR PURPOSE

Do you remember the opening credits of *The Jetsons*, where, after getting ready for the day, each member of the family pops into a little spaceship and scoots off into the world to go about their business? I picture each post we write, conversation we have, and speech we give as one of those spaceships—each one containing a piece of our core purpose that's flying out to parts unknown to make an impact.

The more we keep our purpose at the forefront of our consciousness, the more it gets infused into how we think, talk, and move through the world—whether you're using your purpose as your subject matter or not. For example, I could get up and give a speech about being authentic (and believe me, I have). This entire book is about being authentic—so it's clearly built on the foundation of my Dig word. But when I talk about community, dating, parenting, health—anything—it's always through the lens of authenticity.

In other words, I don't want to give you the impression that once you uncover your Dig word and purpose, that's all you get to talk about for the rest of your life. Rather, all the work you've just done will infuse whatever topic you're talking about with your own authentic flair and authority.

One of my most intimidating and simultaneously inspiring clients is named Ryan Harris. This guy is a force of nature. He's a Super Bowl champion—a six-foot-five NFL offensive lineman with a decade-long career and a deep, magnetic belief in what's possible. Growing up biracial and advancing his sports career against all odds, his life was full of grit and perseverance.

I remember sitting in my downtown Boulder office, listening to Ryan's story. The whole time I could see a hawk circling above the skyline behind him. I'm obsessed with hawks (especially red-tailed hawks), so I couldn't help but notice it. But I'd never seen one in downtown Boulder—so it absolutely seemed like a sign when we landed on Ryan's Dig word: "Beyond"!

After the Dig, Ryan took this frequency of "Beyond" back into the world to craft his speaking career around helping others overcome their limiting beliefs and reach their full potential. He challenged people to go further, be bolder, and act faster than they ever thought possible. His way with words is so powerful that even the most insecure person in the rooms he speaks in ends up leaving feeling like a super hero.

As you might imagine, there was a whole lot of big energy at my Dig HQ that day, so I headed to the yoga studio afterward to decompress. The yoga teacher was a sweet Southern woman in a pastel yoga outfit and pearls. So imagine my surprise when she turned around to reveal an enormous tattoo on her back that read: *BEYOND*.

The synchronicities just kept coming!

Ryan's story is a powerful reminder that your purpose doesn't end with you when you live from a place of alignment. It ripples out and the world reflects it back in ways that are almost eerie in their accuracy.

And when I think about what it means to live a purpose-driven life, Ryan's story is one I return to again and again. It's not about what you've accomplished—it's about how far you're willing to go and how many people you're willing to take with you.

TAKEAWAYS

- Purpose is energizing. When people uncover their Dig word, it often compels them to act—whether that means starting a business, launching a creative project, or simply having more intentional conversations.

- You don't have to share your purpose loudly to make an impact. Living from your truth might look like writing a book or launching a talk—but it can also mean quietly shifting how you show up in everyday interactions.

- Your message ecosystem is the living, breathing map of how your purpose shows up in your job, creative outlets, content, relationships, and more—each radiating from your Dig word.

- Not all areas of your ecosystem will check every box—and that's okay. The goal is balance, not perfection. Some parts will feed your soul, some will align with your purpose, some will pay the bills, and the best ones will do all three.

SOMEBODY'S GOTTA GO FIRST

My friend Ruthie was obsessed with Wonder Woman. When she was diagnosed with stage IV terminal colon cancer in her mid-thirties, her friends lined up to support her in any way they could, including creating a Wonder Woman–themed Facebook page for her and taking turns running errands and spending time with her.

When my day came to take Ruthie to her chemotherapy session, I thought it might bring a smile to her face if I showed up dressed as Wonder Woman. I put on the whole getup—leotard, boots, bracelets, and of course, a Lasso of Truth. On my way to her house, Ruthie's husband called and asked if I could stop by Starbucks to pick up her favorite drink. Of course! I was dressed ridiculously, so I figured I'd just use the drive-through. But when I pulled into the parking lot, there was no drive-through option.

I started to sweat.

It was one thing to walk into a clinic dressed like this, where it would be clear I was there to cheer someone up. It was another to walk into a public space looking like a lost singing telegram. My pulse raced at the uncomfortable thought.

But I was determined that Ruthie get her coffee, so I parked the car and gathered my courage. My heart pounding, I pulled open the door and strode into the store. People gaped at me at first, then broke into smiles. I even got a few high fives. Slowly, I started to relax.

As I stood in line to order Ruthie's coffee, a small woman with big brown eyes walked up. Sweetly grasping my hands she said, "I have to know why you're dressed like that."

Well, that's a loaded question.

Was this one of those times when people ask you how you're doing, but they don't really want to know the messy truth? Should I make up something cheerful to keep the good vibes up? Or was I really about to ruin this woman's day by telling her the heartbreaking reason I was dressed up?

It doesn't always feel safe to let people see our beautiful, complicated, real selves. But my whole human operating system is based on feeling free to be authentic. And that means giving others space to be authentic, too. I have to model for others what authenticity can look like and give them permission to try it, right? Slowly but surely, this is how we can change our whole culture for the better.

So I asked my grounding question—"How real do I want to be?"—and remembered that if I wanted others to have the space to be authentic and vulnerable, I needed to go first.

I chose to answer the woman truthfully. "I have an amazing friend going through an epic cancer battle," I said. "It's crushing my heart, but my friend absolutely loves Wonder Woman. I just want to do one little thing to bring her joy today as I take her to chemo."

The woman looked at me and said, "You have no idea what you just did for me. Thank you." Then she turned and walked out the door.

I don't know where she was going, or what she was going through. I don't know why she felt compelled to talk to me in that

Starbucks line, or why that interaction was powerful for her. All I know is that being our authentic selves and communicating our messages is risky, but always worth it.

It's worth it because it feels good to be authentic. It's worth it because it makes us stronger each time we choose to show up with our whole truth instead of hiding it. But it's *also* worth it because when we say, "You know what? I'll be real. I'll be vulnerable. I'll go first," it opens the door for those around us to tap into their truth, too.

I don't know what the woman in the coffee shop did after we spoke. Maybe she dialed up a friend and reached out for help. Maybe she walked back home and chose to have a hard conversation she'd been avoiding. Maybe she was going through cancer, too, and I brightened her spirits enough to keep fighting for another day. All I know is that because I chose to share my truth, it gave her the opportunity to tap into something that might have otherwise been left buried.

One of the most gratifying things about Digging clients is seeing how much power they discover within themselves when they reach epic clarity about who they are. That power needs an outlet. It needs to shine. And it would be a tragedy to squander the opportunity to achieve anything less than our full potential—we all have so much to offer.

It will take courage to speak your truth, just as it took courage for me to speak mine in that coffee shop. But every time we do, we start a chain reaction, our truth a spark that ignites the souls around us in an ever-increasing circle of authentic humans who are empowered to shine their own best light back out into the world.

The course of history doesn't always shift on huge battles or cataclysmic pandemics. Sometimes it shifts because one person decided to go first.

People like Rosa Parks, who kicked off the Montgomery bus boycott with a simple act of honest defiance. Harvey Milk, who lived his truth as one of the first openly gay elected officials in the US and helped push the door open for acceptance. Greta Thunberg, who initiated a global climate conversation by protesting alone outside Swedish parliament. Tarana Burke, whose commitment to speaking openly about assault created space for thousands of women to say, "Me too."

You don't have to start a new movement to live in your authentic truth. But if we want a world where everyone is free to be exactly who they are, somebody's gotta go first.

Why not you?

BEING AUTHENTIC—SAFELY

I want to pause for a moment and acknowledge the heartbreaking truth that being your authentic self is safer for some people than for others.

I'm a cisgender white woman. I have friends who are immigrants, transgender, Muslim, Black, queer—and I've heard their stories. I've listened as they told me what it feels like to walk through the world with a target on their back and how "just be yourself" feels like a luxury not everyone is afforded. And even those of us who pass more easily in the dominant culture might not feel safe to be our most authentic selves around our families, at work, or in public.

I vividly remember preparing to speak at a big tech company, when one of their employees—a jovial woman with wonderful big energy—asked what I was going to talk about.

"I'm going to talk about bringing your authentic self to work," I said.

She laughed and replied, "If I bring my authentic self to work, I'm getting fired."

And I get it. Being our authentic selves isn't going to work well in all the settings of life. You might not feel safe to authentically express your gender at work. You may not feel able to openly celebrate your culture, speak in your natural accent, thrive in your disability, or be comfortable in your immigration status. That's the sad truth of this world, and I'm not asking you to put yourself at risk.

I want to be clear. Being authentic doesn't have to mean putting yourself in danger.

It doesn't mean baring your soul in unsafe environments or sharing everything with everyone. And it definitely doesn't mean ignoring the very real consequences that some people face when their truth runs counter to societal norms, power structures, or deeply ingrained bias.

This goes back to our earlier discussion of authenticity and transparency. Remember that authenticity is about alignment—about living from your values and truth. Transparency is about disclosure. They're not the same thing. You can be deeply authentic without disclosing a single personal detail. You can walk in truth without making yourself a target. You can honor who you are *and* what you need to feel safe.

Amal Kassir is one of my clients and also one of the most incredible slam poets I've ever seen. She's a small woman who seems eternally youthful, but when she starts in on a poem, she mows the room down with her power. Her Dig word is "Choose."

She's also Muslim and wears a hijab. She grew up in the US, with family from Syria, and in her TEDx Talk, "The Muslim on the Airplane," Amal shares what it was like to come of age as a Muslim in America after the September 11 attacks—especially when flying, where her hijab makes her immediately noticeable.

Onstage as a slam poet and speaker, Amal has honed her truth until it is as sharp as a knife. She doesn't shy away from making her audience uncomfortable. She doesn't let them look away from the devastating reality of the war-torn Middle East or the hate she's experienced as a Muslim in the US.

But when she's on a plane?

Standing up and delivering a spitfire slam poem might be an incredibly satisfying and authentic way to clap back at everyone giving her dirty looks. Is that a safe way to be authentic, though? Probably not. So Amal *chose* something different—but equally real.

She carries a package of mints, and at the end of the flight, she pulls it out of her bag and offers one to the people around her. As she says in her TEDx Talk, "After a four-hour seven a.m. flight, everyone has bad breath. So almost anyone is willing to take the mint from the Muslim on the airplane."

Offering a mint might not seem like a vulnerable act of authenticity, but when you've spent the last several hours being glared at, scrutinized, avoided, and selected for "random" security screenings, offering an olive branch is a bold choice. And when Amal chooses to take that first step, when she authentically *goes first*, her seatmates often reflect her choice in offering their name or an offhand comment about the flight or the weather, ask her questions, and ultimately transform the environment of fear and suspicion into one of shared understanding and connection. By taking the initiative, Amal not only challenges the stereotypes projected onto her; she invites others to see beyond their preconceived notions and walk away with a positive memory of someone they once feared.

Sometimes, authenticity looks like speaking your truth on a stage. Other times, it looks like whispering it to a trusted friend or writing it in a journal. All of that is okay. You don't owe anyone your story. But you do owe yourself the self-knowledge and self-respect it takes to own your truth in all its messy wholeness. But ultimately, Digging is your choice (and it's certainly not for everyone).

When you're living in alignment with who *you* are, in the way *you* define it, it's powerful as hell.

YOUR DECISION POINT

Remember that briefcase we talked about in chapter 2? The one that contains everything you need to ace every meeting, identify common ground, communicate more clearly, and become a better human, parent, partner, and friend?

You've got it in your hand now. What you do with it is up to you.

I've given you the step-by-step instructions, the examples, the stories, the how-tos. I've gone first in sharing my own truth to make space and inspire you to tap into yours. And now I want to leave you with a question.

What are *you* going to do?

Because let's be honest. How many times have we gone to a retreat or taken a workshop or read a book like this and walked away feeling lit up … only to do absolutely nothing with it? It happens all the time. We get inspired, we highlight passages, maybe even take a few notes. But then life comes rushing back in, and all that insight ends up tucked away in some mental file.

And listen—if that's where you are, I get it. Maybe you're feeling a little intimidated. Maybe you've got a story running in the background that says, *"This isn't for me,"* or *"I'm not ready."* Maybe it's just not the right season. That's okay.

But I also want to gently challenge you to choose action.

Right. Now.

I'm not saying you have to go out and complete the full Dig process tomorrow. I'm not saying you need to shout your truth from the rooftops. I'm just inviting you to think differently—to tune in to the frequencies we've been talking about, to start noticing what resonates, to become just a little more open. Because when you begin to see the themes that run through your life—the lessons, the patterns, the invitations—you begin to understand that maybe, just maybe, those things aren't random. Maybe they're here to illuminate something important about your purpose.

And here's the secret: choosing to open up, even just a little, when you'd rather stay closed? That's power. Real power.

So wherever you are on your journey, I just want you to know this: You don't have to do it all. But you *do* have a choice. You can let this remain an idea, or you can let it become a practice.

What's it going to be?

APPENDIX
CRAFTING YOUR MESSAGE

Throughout this book, we've talked about how to tap into the core of your purpose and how the clarity you get will help bring your message to life. My expertise is in public speaking and coaching leaders through turning their purpose into a well-crafted message that lands with (and moves) their audiences, so I wanted to leave one final practical gift to help you find your own clarity of message.

This appendix is built around my framework for creating a speech that deeply connects with your audience because it's built around your authentic truth. Whether or not you intend to ever get up onstage, going through this exercise is a fantastic way to clarify what you've learned through the course of this book and integrate it into your daily life.

If you've been doing the work as you've read along, you should have a pretty good grasp of your Dig word, your human operating system, and your purpose—not just what you want to say but why it matters. Now we'll build on that to help you write a speech that's powerful, unique, and perfectly you.

Whether you're preparing for a keynote, a TEDx Talk, a team meeting, a podcast interview, or just a hard conversation where you need to make your truth known, this four-part recipe for a powerful speech will help you craft a message that lands:

1. Reflect on what you're trying to achieve and make a plan to get there.
2. Discover and organize your content, drawing from media, lessons, and your own personal stories.
3. Shape that content using a storyboard format so you can fine-tune your flow and emotional impact.
4. Finally, script it out so you can embody your message and deliver it with impact.

This isn't a blueprint or a fill-in-the-blank template to help you write a speech that sounds like everyone else's. I really don't believe there's a formula for a successful delivery of your message. To me, the act of sharing your truth with an audience is much too sacred to put in a restrictive box. Instead, what I'm going to give you is a flow that enables you to craft your own authentic message, whatever the context.

Sharing your truth with an audience isn't just dumping a bunch of information on them. It's a journey—one that you go through first, then guide your audience through.

Let's dive in.

STEP 1: REFLECTION

Before we write a single word, we need to understand our why. And I don't just mean your larger why—all the work that you just did in the Dig. I mean why get up on this stage, make this presentation at work, write this blog post, or have this conversation? Why talk to this audience? What do you have to offer them? What are they showing up to hear? How can you make this super relatable? How can you bring your most creative and authentic self and make people's lives better as a result of spending their precious time listening to you?

Unfortunately, this is a step that people often skip. You can normally spot presenters who haven't done prep work. Their stories don't land, they ramble instead of making an incisive point, and they leave you feeling kind of…unimpressed. They didn't start by aligning their message with their audience's needs.

You need to understand yourself, and the event, to know how your message will land with your audience. When I work with speaking clients one-on-one or in workshops, the first thing we do is go through a Dig. Which means you can rejoice—you're already ahead of the game! Now let's turn our attention to the event itself. It's time to answer some questions.

Tip: Head to erinweed.com/justoneword to download my speech-planning worksheet.

Logistics

Let's start by getting a handle on the basics of the who, what, when, why, and where of the event. If you're sharing your message in an interview, what's the background of why you were invited to the program? If you're making a presentation at work, what's the context? If you're writing a book, what are the parameters around it, and who will your audience be?

If the event is a speech, this list of questions is great to have in front of you when you're talking with the event organizer. You can use it to guide your conversation and get all the information you need. Here are some basic questions to ask:

- What's the occasion for the speech or presentation?
- Where is the event?
- Where will you be speaking?
- What's the date and time of the event?
- When will your speech be taking place?

- How long will your speech be?
- What topic is the organizer expecting you to speak on?
- Why were you asked to present?
- How big is the audience?
- Who will be in the audience? (Think of both demographics and psychographics.)
- What technology will you have? (Will there be a microphone, projector, and screen?)
- What should you wear?

All this information will help you shape your material. A ten-minute talk is a different beast from a fifty-minute workshop. A blog post is different from a book. Asking your boss for permission to pursue a project is different from making your case via a PowerPoint presentation to the entire team (even though the bones might be the same—I'll talk you through my "slinky speech" method later in this appendix).

Similarly, when and who matter. A lunchtime talk or casual podcast chat will have a different energy from an evening talk or formal studio interview. While audience size isn't always that significant, it's important to know because you'll show up differently for ten people than you will for a hundred.

Introspection

Now let's spend some time thinking about the impact sharing your message will have on you and your audience. Ask:

- What do you want the audience to think?
- What do you want the audience to feel?

- What do you want the audience to do as a result of hearing your message?
- What feelings do you have about sharing your message? (Fears, hopes, doubts, etc.)

You may notice that the sequence of think, feel, and do is exactly what we talked about earlier in Head-Heart-Core. That's not a coincidence. Head-Heart-Core is a great way to think about not just the effect you want to have on your audience but also how to develop the flow of your message.

Getting clear on how you're feeling is important, too. Acknowledge if you're feeling nervous, excited, unsure, or hopeful. We're going to be as authentic as possible here, and being honest about your feelings is a perfect way to get started.

Content

Finally, what are the basics you need to cover? It can be easy to get wrapped up in the excitement of the next few steps, so take the time now to jot down the building blocks of your message:

- Who do you need to thank or acknowledge? (Sponsors, hosts, previous presenters, your teammates, etc.)
- What are the most important points you need to cover to share your message?
- What are some stories you can tell about this topic?
- What are some jokes or things the audience may find amusing about the topic?
- Is there anything else that should be included in your message?

STEP 2: GATHERING CONTENT

Now that we've got a grasp on the what of your message—the logistics, the desired impact, and the required content—it's time to start gathering up your building blocks. I like to think of it like building a Lego house without a kit.

First you have to gather up all the Lego bricks you have so you can sort through them and figure out what color the house is going to be, how tall it'll be, and whether it will have turrets, cannons, palm trees, or any other fun features.

Each individual Lego brick is a piece of content: a story, joke, call to action, question, challenge, thesis, argument, or any other self-contained idea. Stacking these bricks is how we're going to craft your message.

In other words, before you start building, you need to figure out what you have to work with.

Go wild in this step! Seriously, don't hold back. The more building blocks the better, so don't get caught up self-editing as you gather material. The goal is to generate ideas with abandon, knowing that some of your best stories and one-liners will come when you've already exhausted the obvious ones.

Think about it this way: For every ten pieces of content you excavate in this step, you'll probably keep one. That takes some of the pressure away, right? Who cares if an idea is good? Just jot it down and keep going. It's only got a one-in-ten chance of making it into your speech anyway, so give yourself the freedom to brainstorm without restraint and throw out anything that doesn't fit.

The great news is that you don't have to actually throw away your unused ideas. This probably isn't the only speech, presentation, or interview you'll ever give. It's probably not the only essay or book you'll write. All the stories, facts, and personal flourishes you dredge up in this step can be used in the future.

Here are some of my favorite methods for extracting content that's real, resonant, and ready to work with. (I've also included a list of content prompts at the end of this section.)

1. Audio Self-Capture

This method is perfect for people who think best while speaking. Print out the list of content prompts at the end of this section, then go for a walk and talk to your phone like it's a podcast mic. Or grab a cup of tea and cozy up on your couch, then press record. You could even take five or ten minutes and sit in your car with a voice memo app if that's the only quiet space you can find.

As you record, don't worry about sounding polished—just talk about your topic like you would with a close friend. Let yourself ramble away and see where you start making connections.

You can transcribe the recording manually, if you prefer—I usually use an online transcription service that lets me upload the audio to generate a transcript. However you get the text, read through it and highlight anything you think might serve you well in this speech.

2. Freewriting

If you're a writer at heart, open a notebook or Google Doc and just let it rip. Set a timer for fifteen or twenty minutes and write without editing or censoring—just let stories or thoughts come forward without judgment. Try to make it through your entire timer without taking your pen off the paper. When you force the words to keep flowing, it can take you to surprising places. The end result is often uncensored, unfiltered thoughts on your subject matter.

If you're having trouble turning off your critical brain, ask yourself this question: What would I write if I were never going to show this to anyone?

3. Interview-Style Discovery

Ask a friend, coach, or collaborator to ask you a series of questions about your subject matter or to take you through the content prompts. This works especially well if you have a conversational processing style.

Sometimes, having someone else ask curious, open-ended questions helps you reveal insights you didn't know you had. And when you ask your interviewer to put themselves in the shoes of your audience, they might come up with questions you wouldn't think to ask yourself.

4. Get Creative

If you're comfortable on-camera, try recording short video clips as if you were talking to your ideal audience. What would you say if you had five minutes to change someone's mind or open their heart? Or maybe you feel more comfortable expressing yourself through painting, music, collage, or some other nonverbal medium.

Choose whatever method helps you remove the blocks, judgments, and filters that are getting in the way of you finding your message.

5. Head-Heart-Core

Go back to the Head-Heart-Core exercise in chapter 3 and use it to access each of those truths about your topic. What do you know or think about this topic (your Head facts)? What do you feel about it (your Heart truths)? And, finally, what do you want to see happen as a result of your talk (your Core desires)?

An effectively crafted message will have a nice balance of all three. When you include all three, you know you're expressing your full truth. You're also more likely to connect with the audience, because you're giving them more entry points into your message. Some people will always click with the intellectual side of your message. Others will connect with the emotional side. And some will be moved when you share your authentic desires.

Content Prompts

- What do you know to be true about <topic>?

- Take a breath. What in your heart needs to be said about <topic>?

- What do you know that others don't about <topic>?

- What are three tips you have for others about <topic>?

- How have you failed in <topic>?

- How does your Dig word relate to <topic>?

- Do you have any jokes or funny stories about <topic>?

- Tell me about three times in your life that <topic> was a thing.

- Is there someone in your life who violates your beliefs on <topic>? What do you wish you could say to that person? No filter!

- How would the world be better if everyone understood <topic>?

- What do you believe or want for the future of <topic>?

- When did <topic> become real for you?

STEP 3: STORYBOARDING

A storyboard is a visual outline of a message that flows with clarity, energy, and purpose. A storyboard helps you figure out the order of your message and how each piece of content contributes to the journey you're taking your audience on.

I like to think of speeches and presentations as roller coasters. The audience is strapped into their seats (probably not literally, but you never know!), and your words are taking them on a ride. There are high points of excitement, jokes, and laughter. There are poignant, serious moments that ask them to be introspective. There are tense, anticipatory climbs followed by looping reversals and twists. And, along with all these dips and drops, there will also be moments of steadiness and consistency and neutrality.

A good message—like a good roller coaster—needs to have a little bit of everything in a flow that's both surprising and satisfying.

For storyboarding, we're going back to the sticky notes. Grab a stack and find a big open surface. It can be a window, a dry-erase board, a television set, your bathroom mirror—even your refrigerator. Anywhere in your house that can hold sticky notes works.

As you gather your physical materials—sticky notes, drawing board, and pens—I also want you to bring your openness and curiosity. This should be fun! When you can tap into that mindset, it'll help keep you going through a process that's not always straightforward. A lot of the storyboarding process involves sitting with your content ideas, staring at sticky notes, and tapping into your Resonance Meter to figure out where it should land. Stay curious and you'll do fine.

The 5-Bucket Framework

The 5-Bucket Framework is the bridge between raw content and a resonant message—a structure that gives your ideas room to move, breathe, and connect. Think of each bucket as a chapter in the emotional and intellectual journey you're creating for your audience. Together, they form a complete arc.

This framework works no matter how long your message is. You can use it to prepare a ten-minute TEDx Talk or a ninety-minute interactive keynote. You can use it in a thousand-word essay or a full-length book. In fact, you can use the same five buckets to develop a message that can be expanded or contracted to fit different scenarios. When I'm coaching speech clients, I call this a slinky speech. These five buckets make up the structure and the skeleton of your message, but what you say within them—and how much time you spend communicating each one—is highly flexible.

Bucket 1: The Invitation

This is your opening. Your chance to grab the audience's attention, build trust, and let them know what kind of ride they're in for. You might be tempted to start with your credentials, your job title, or the outline of what you're about to say. Don't. Save that for later (or skip it entirely). The first bucket should always be about the person listening rather than the person speaking. Your audience wants to know: *Why should I care?* and *How is this relevant to me?*

Begin with something that earns attention and builds connection: a personal story, a bold question, a surprising statement, or even a clear intention. I told you about Ash Beckham in chapter 1 and her talk about coming out of your closet. Her opening lines were "I am going to talk to you tonight about coming out of the closet. And not in the traditional sense, not just the gay closet. I think we all have closets. Your closet may be telling someone you love her for the first time. Or telling someone that you're pregnant. Or telling someone you have cancer. Or any of the other hard conversations we have throughout our lives. All the closet is, is a hard conversation."

When you hear an introduction like that, you know exactly what you're in for. A good Bucket 1 sets the tone, opens a loop the rest of the message will close, and grounds the audience in your intention. Think of it like opening a door and saying, "Come in. I've got something meaningful to share." Then tell them what it is.

Buckets 2, 3, and 4: The Takeaways

The three buckets between your introduction and your conclusion are your takeaways. I've found that three main takeaways is about the maximum that your audience (and you) can hold on to, and organizing your supporting information around those takeaways helps the audience remember way more than they would with a random string of stories.

In her classic book, *The Pyramid Principle: Logic in Writing and Thinking*, Barbara Minto outlines her Minto Pyramid Principle— basically, the idea that humans naturally categorize and group the information we receive, so your audience is way more likely to retain what you're saying if you organize your communications in that logical order.[1]

For example, if I tell you to go to the grocery store and give you a list of fifteen things in random order, you might remember half of them. You're way more likely to remember them all if I tell you, "Tonight, we're having a salad with dinner so I need salad greens, radishes, a cucumber, and dressing. We'll also need something fun for dessert, like ice cream! Tomorrow morning, we'll need half-and-half for coffee, and milk for the cereal."

When I give you the logical reason I'm asking for those things and group them together, you're able to go to the grocery store with the understanding of what I am actually asking you to prepare for, and you will retain that information more clearly.

That's what we're doing with your three middle buckets. Remember Ryan Harris from chapter 11? He has three main takeaways as he guides audiences through his framework for mastering your mindset. "I am. I can. I will." So easy, a kindergartener can remember it (and probably implement it, too).

Bucket 5: The Call Forward

If the first bucket is about connecting with the person listening, the final bucket is about what you want them to do. It's your call to action. When your audience steps out into the lobby after your speech, who do you want them to call or text? When your meeting with your boss is over, what do you want their next step to be? When someone finishes reading your essay, what do you want them to say they just learned?

Go back to your speech-planning worksheet and revisit these questions:

- What do you want the audience to think?
- What do you want the audience to feel?
- What do you want the audience to do as a result of hearing your message?

You can close with a story that echoes your opening. You can issue a call to action, a rhetorical question, or a single sentence that will echo in their heads for days. Whatever you choose, make it intentional and connect it to the ultimate takeaway of your speech.

Putting It All Together

Let's take a look at my TEDx Talk, "Dare to Be Authentic," to see the 5-Bucket Framework in action. (Give it a quick watch if you haven't seen it already.)

Bucket 1 (Introduction): I start off my introduction with the story I told in chapter 3 about working as an extra for a reality TV show. I tie it to my central theme by sharing what I learned about authenticity and use it to frame my central question: *"How real do you want to be?"* I end that first bucket with a punch line about questioning our own authenticity and transparency.

Bucket 2 (Context): Next, I go into Head content. Notice that I start this bucket with a definition to get everybody on the same page. This is especially important if you're talking about something whose meaning people might disagree on. In my case, I define transparency and authenticity and talk about the difference between the two. This sets up the context for the problem I'm going to talk about in Bucket 3.

Taking time to clarify and define terms builds trust with your audience. I liken this to being a river-rafting guide. Your audience is much more likely to trust that they're in good hands if you spend a few minutes up front explaining the safety features and rules.

Bucket 3 (Problem): In this bucket, I connect with my audience emotionally by sharing the relatable story of feeling disconnected at a networking event. We've all been there, right? So we can all identify with that experience and how painful it is. This is a Heart bucket, getting my audience to feel the universal problem of authentically connecting with others. I present the problem of my central question, *"How real do you want to be?"* in an emotionally charged way, setting us up nicely to solve it in the next bucket.

Bucket 4 (Solution): This is where I teach the concept of Head-Heart-Core and help people understand how it enables us to speak our truth. Because this was a ten-minute talk, I didn't have a ton of time to dive into the exercise—but I did my best to share how it increases our connection with those around us. This is what I want my audience to take away—it shows them my desire that people relate better to others, even in awkward situations.

Bucket 5 (Call to Action): Finally, I share the story of being dressed as Wonder Woman in Starbucks, how that awkward scenario illustrates that we always have a choice to show up authentically, and how that creates an impact on others. That story works really well because it makes people laugh, cry, think, and then leave wanting to make awesome choices about how they're showing up in the world. My call to action is for my audience to walk out that door daring to be authentic.

The Chorus

As you collect your materials, you'll probably also start to see a common theme or thread emerging from the stories. I call this a chorus. Sometimes this is a line you repeat multiple times in order to drive a point home. Sometimes it's a question you explore throughout, or an issue you look at from different angles.

In my speech, you'll notice that I touch on my chorus (*"How real do you want to be?"*) in every bucket. No matter how out of left field a story is, when I tie it into my chorus, the audience trusts that I'm taking them on a clear, well-planned journey. Having a chorus gives them the theme, sure. But it also establishes audience trust.

As a side note, you'll also probably notice that I shared all the stories from my speech in this book, in roughly the same order. See what I mean about a slinky speech? When you find a flow that works, it can be just as powerful in a ten-minute talk, a ninety-minute workshop, or a book. If you're creating something longer, you fill it with more detail, research, and examples. If it's shorter, you keep the same bones; you just make it a bit leaner.

Create Your Storyboard

Grab your sticky notes and your pen—it's time to create your own storyboard. Start by writing Buckets 1–5 on five sticky notes and put them up on the wall in order. Then begin jotting down all the stories, facts, questions, and other content you dug up in the last step and stick them on your flat surface, grouping them into the five buckets without worrying too much about order.

As you start to dial in the structure of your message, you might subtract sticky notes or brainstorm new ones, depending on what comes up for you and how much time you're trying to fill.

As a quick rule of thumb, a shorter message should have one main story or point per bucket, with a few supporting ideas thrown in to help make your point. A longer one will have multiple stories to illustrate the theme of each bucket. But at this point, your main focus is on organizing and categorizing. You can cut or add later.

It might take a few days before you feel done, and that's okay. Sit with it for as long as you need until you feel good about the flow. And *do not* move on until you're done with your storyboard! You might be eager to jump ahead and start writing, but let me tell you: I've seen, through years of experience both giving and coaching speeches, that it's much easier to change things at the storyboard phase than it is to edit a written speech or a complete book draft. You'll save yourself a huge headache if you sit with this step until it's fully done.

STEP 4: WRITE YOUR CONTENT

If you're presenting your message as an essay or a book, this is an obvious step. But even if you're going to be speaking your message aloud, take time to script it out first. I know this is the part some of you might shrug off—especially if you're pretty comfortable just speaking off the cuff. You might be thinking, *But I don't want to sound like a robot! I just want to get up there and talk.*

I hear you. But here's the thing: Scripting is not about memorizing every single word and reciting it before an audience. It's about making sure all the hard work you've done truly lands with your audience.

The best thing you can do for your future self on the stage *and* for your audience is to take the time to craft a script, then learn to deliver it in a way that doesn't seem wooden or over-rehearsed. The process of working on your script prepares you for the stage. So think of this as an investment in your stage performance—even if you're the type who feels comfortable speaking extemporaneously in front of an audience.

From a more pragmatic perspective, scripting also helps you keep track of time. It's simple math. If you're slated for a ten-minute talk, you should have about fifteen hundred words in your script. If you end up with a five-thousand-word draft, you've got a real problem. (For a rough guide, go to speechinminutes.com.)

Now, I'm just going to say this again: *Don't* skip to this part if your storyboard isn't solid. Don't move forward until you feel really good about your buckets and your flow. If you start writing too early, before your structure is set, you'll just create more work for yourself down the line—trust me on this. The exception is if you do your best processing through writing. If writing is the best way for you to think, then sure, go ahead and write to discover. Just know that you may need to do extensive rewrites later, once your structure is clearer.

Here are some tips to keep in mind as you write:

Remember Your Chorus

What's your theme? Your refrain? The point you're trying to hammer home? In my TEDx Talk, I kept asking the question, *"How real do you want to be?"* That idea showed up in every single bucket, and even if I didn't say those exact words, it was the thread that tied the whole thing together.

Write Clearly

Always err on the side of being clear rather than being clever. Especially in a speech, you want to keep things short and snappy. I break my script into short paragraphs or single lines, partly because it's easier to rehearse, and partly because short, intentional sentences often land with the audience better. If you find your first draft is filled with long, complex sentences, keep revising until you find a clearer way to say it.

One tip—whether you're presenting your message live or writing for readers—is to periodically read your draft aloud. That's a great way to catch those long, rambling sentences that pull readers out of the moment. (And which no one would ever actually say.)

Embrace the Shitty First Draft

We've already talked about the power of the shitty first draft. (Thanks again, Anne Lamott.) When you're crafting your message, lean into it! Open a blank document, label your five buckets, and start dumping in the content from your sticky notes. Don't worry about transitions yet. Don't worry about flow. Just get it out of your head and into the world.

Hone Your Transitions

As you revise your draft, you'll start refining the transitions between your stories, facts, and refrains so that they flow. This is important no matter the medium of your message, but in my experience transitions are one of the most overlooked parts of speaking—and they make or break the energy in a room. When you don't have a smooth handoff from one idea to the next, it creates an awkwardness that pulls people out of the experience. So, even if your transition is just three words, make it intentional.

Sharpen Your Humor

There are very few messages that wouldn't benefit from a touch of humor—and most speeches rely on it pretty heavily, even if the topic isn't naturally comedic. It's hard to know exactly what jokes will land with an audience until you're delivering them, but scripting is a good place to try them out and see how it goes. If you're writing an essay or a book and not sure how a bit of humor is working, ask a beta reader to give you feedback.

Kill Your Darlings

The hardest part about writing out your message is knowing that the more you tighten and refine it, the tougher your decisions get about what material ends up on the cutting-room floor. While your shitty first draft is all about getting everything out on the page, you need to be ruthless as you revise. That vignette about your kid's stuffed sheep is adorable, but does it serve the story? That cool fact about pangolins is fascinating, but is it actually important to your point? If the answer is no, throw it in a file to use in a later piece of content.

Color-Code Your Script

One of my favorite tips for speakers and presenters is to color-code your script. This makes it much easier to scan and memorize and helps you remember your pacing as you deliver the speech. Here's the code I use:

- **Regular black text** = just your normal script. Important, but doesn't need to be emphasized.
- **Bold black** = things you want to emphasize. Maybe you need to slow down here or speak more firmly.
- **Orange** = slides or visuals—anything your audience is seeing while you're speaking. Could be a prop, a movie clip, or a slide on the screen behind you. If you like, you can grab a thumbnail of your slide and put it in your script as a reminder, too.
- **Pink** = *Don't mess this up.* These are the lines you need to memorize. They're often short or punchy, like your chorus or repeated phrase—something you want to nail every time.

Rehearse Your Message

Whether you're getting up onstage in front of hundreds of people, making a presentation to your boss, or pitching your spouse on a vacation spot, it pays to rehearse your message. The goal here isn't to memorize your script word for word. Rather, it's to get your stories, beats, jokes, chorus, and overall points down so well that you can deliver your message in an authentic, heartfelt way.

Remember: The World Needs Your Passion

I find scripting to be the most enjoyable part of the speech-development process, but I know that's not the same for everyone.

Some people love storyboarding. Others can't wait to start practicing. I've seen people get stuck, become frustrated, or want to throw it all out the window and walk away for good—at every phase.

Which, any writer will tell you, is simply part of the creative process. No matter how much skill you have and no matter how passionate you are, writing your script is going to be a creative wrestling match. But you've done the work. You've reflected on what you're trying to create. You've gathered your content. You've created a storyboard. You can do this.

If you start getting frustrated or overwhelmed during script writing, don't worry. It doesn't mean you shouldn't be speaking or that you're a fraud. It just means you're putting something creative and vulnerable out in the world, and that's extremely tough.

It's all part of the practice, and it's absolutely worth fighting through. You may even come to enjoy it.

After all, the world needs your message.

RESOURCES

My website, erinweed.com/justoneword, is full of resources to get you started on unearthing your purpose and message. My team and I are constantly adding new content to help you "Dig yourself" and get the epic clarity of your own life purpose and message. Subscribe to get access to free training videos and other bonus materials.

ACKNOWLEDGMENTS

This book exists because of the many amazing humans who have trusted me with their stories. Over the years, I've had the privilege of Digging more than a thousand leaders, seekers, and changemakers. To everyone I have had the honor and privilege to work with, I say thank you. This is *our* book.

To my literary agent Brandi Bowles—thank you for seeing the potential in the Dig after just one phone call, and for bringing it to life.

To my publishers Renée Sedliar at GCP Balance and Drummond Moir at Atlantic Books in the UK—thank you for helping this message amplify across the world. In addition, I'd like to thank the team at Balance: Nana Twumasi, Terri Sirma, Tamara Coleman, Nan Rittenhouse, Jessica McKenzie, Nzinga Temu, Luria Rittenberg, and Eileen Chetti.

To my writing and editing partners—Jessie Kwak, Jennifer Kasius, and Stephanie Land—I deeply appreciate your expertise and commitment to your craft. Thank you for helping bring my life's work to the page.

To my fellow authors and mentors—especially Jonathan Fields, Rosalind Wiseman, and Sam Horn—thank you for your wisdom and encouragement.

To my girlfriends—Emily, Heather, Tessa, and Angie—I'll never forget you rollin' up to my house the night I got the book deal, blasting music and confetti out of your car. Everyone deserves a cheer squad like you.

To my late bestie George Morris—this book is all your fault, in the most beautiful way. You believed in the Dig since day one, and your word, "Soul," continues to guide me from the stars.

To my bonus kids, Kyle and Jillian Morris, your dad's essence is imprinted on every page—just as he lives on in both of you. Mushin Kaizen!

To my parents, JoAnne and Wyman Weed—you are masters at creating safe spaces for people to be their most authentic selves. Thank you for giving me roots and wings.

To my kids, Miles and Phoebe Lacis—thank you for supporting me unconditionally through all the peaches and pits of life. We're an incredible team, always. Mama Hawk loves you fiercely.

And finally, to Dann Albright—thank you for teaching me the beautiful complexity of being "all the things." You are my editor, my best friend, my guardian, and my greatest love. Together, anything is possible. And to think we're just getting started…

NOTES

Introduction

1. Marguerite Ward, "How Each of These 5 Highly-Successful People Overcame Their Quarter-Life Crisis," CNBC, June 22, 2017, https://www.cnbc.com/2017/06/22/how-6-highly-successful-people-overcame-their-quarter-life-crises.html; Oliver C. Robinson, Gordon R. T. Wright, and Jonathan A. Smith, "The Holistic Phase Model of Early Adult Crisis," Birkbeck University of London, n.d., https://eprints.bbk.ac.uk/id/eprint/6706/2/6706.pdf.

2. "The Deloitte Global 2023 Gen Z & Millennial Survey," May 23, 2023, https://www.deloitte.com/nz/en/issues/work/gen-z-millennial-survey-2023.html; Destinee Adams, "Gen Z Workers Are Exhausted—and Seeking Solutions," NPR, *Morning Edition*, May 26, 2023, https://www.npr.org/2023/05/26/1178332514/tips-gen-z-workers-burn-out.

3. Sherry Walling, "3 Insights from the First Large-Scale Study on Burnout and Entrepreneurs," Entrepreneur, March 22, 2023, https://www.entrepreneur.com/living/3-insights-from-the-first-large-scale-study-on-burnout-and/447394.

4. Martin Obschonka, Ignacio Pavez, Teemu Kautonen, Ewald Kibler, Katariina Salmela-Aro, and Joakim Wincent, "Job Burnout and Work Engagement in Entrepreneurs: How the Psychological Utility of Entrepreneurship Drives Healthy Engagement," *Journal of Business Venturing* 38, no. 2 (2023): 106272, https://www.sciencedirect.com/science/article/pii/S0883902622000842?via%3Dihub; Walling, "3 Insights."

5. Walling, "3 Insights"; Jessica Stillman, "Research: Entrepreneurs Are Happier and Healthier Than Employees," Inc., May 23, 2017, https://www.inc.com/jessica-stillman/research-entrepreneurs-are-happier-and-healthier-than-employees.html.

6. Chloe Donelan, "Gen Z in the Workplace: How Should Companies Adapt?," Johns Hopkins University, n.d., https://imagine.jhu.edu/blog/2023/04/18/gen-z-in-the-workplace-how-should-companies-adapt/.

7. Kathy Bloomgarden, "Gen Z and the End of Work as We Know It," World Economic Forum, May 19, 2022, https://www.weforum.org/agenda/2022/05/gen-z-don-t-want-to-work-for-you-here-s-how-to-change-their-mind/.

8. Ralph van den Bosch and Toon W. Taris, "Authenticity at Work: Development and Validation of an Individual Authenticity Measure at Work," *Journal of Happiness*

Studies 15 (2014): 1–18, https://link.springer.com/article/10.1007/s10902-013-9413-3.

9. Carl Jung, *Memories, Dreams, Reflections* (Pantheon Books, 1963).

Chapter 2

1. Gerd Gigerenzer, *The Intelligence of Intuition* (Cambridge University Press, 2023), p. 3.

2. Gavin de Becker, *The Gift of Fear* (Dell, 1998), p. 25.

3. Annie Jacobsen, "The U.S. Military Believes People Have a Sixth Sense," *Time*, April 3, 2017.

4. Joe Dispenza, *Breaking the Habit of Being Yourself* (Hay House, 2013).

Chapter 4

1. "The 'Thinking' Production System: TPS as a Winning Strategy for Developing People in the Global Manufacturing Environment," Public Affairs Division, Toyota Motor Corporation, October 8, 2003, https://www.scribd.com/document/479142125/The-Toyota-Production-System-articles-2-doc.

Chapter 7

1. Anita Stubenrauch, "I Wrote Apple's Credo 6 Years Ago—Here's Why It's Still Relevant," Medium, July 6, 2022, https://medium.com/cause-effect/i-wrote-apples-credo-6-years-ago-here-s-why-it-s-still-relevant-b2525521372e.

Appendix

1. Barbara Minto, *The Pyramid Principle: Logic in Writing and Thinking* (Financial Times/Prentice Hall, 2010).

INDEX

ABOUT THE AUTHOR

Erin Weed is a leadership coach, keynote speaker, and creator of the Dig®, a method that helps people excavate their life stories, identify their Core truths, and distill their purpose down to just one word.

Since 2012, she has guided thousands of leaders, founders, and changemakers to clarify their message, own their power, and communicate with unwavering authenticity. Her work has shaped best-selling books, viral TEDx Talks, major company pivots, and the personal breakthroughs that alter the course of one's life.

Erin began her career in public relations in Chicago before moving to New York City to produce documentaries—a path that sharpened her instinct for story, truth, and human complexity. In 2001, after the murder of a college friend, she founded Girls Fight Back, a personal safety education company. GFB went on to reach over a million people at live events worldwide and was later acquired.

Erin is a sought-after coach and thought leadership advisor, known for her direct guidance, intuitive insights, and ability to help people articulate ideas that genuinely evolve society. Together with her partner, Dann Albright, their company offers coaching and training programs to help leaders align with their purpose and share their message with the masses.

Longtime residents of Colorado, Erin and Dann live with their two teenagers and adorable dogs.